FULLY INCLUDED~

Stories to Inspire Inclusion
for children with Down syndrome
and other special needs

Michelle and Stacy Tetschner

Fully Included~Stories to Inspire Inclusion for children with Down syndrome and other special needs.
©2018, Michelle and Stacy Tetschner

Published in the United States by Michelle and Stacy Tetschner

For more information or to order additional copies of this book visit www. fullyincluded.com

Library of Congress Cataloging-in-Publication Data
Fully Included – Stories To Inspire Inclusion/Michelle and Stacy Tetschner

ISBN - 978–0–578–41831–5 (print)
ISBN - 978–0–578–42150–6 (ebook)

Contents

~SECTION 2: INSPIRING CATHOLIC STORIES~

~SECTION 3: RESOURCES~

Foreword

As the co-author of this book it was my goal to share my passion for inclusion. As the idea of the book grew, I was blessed that people with the same passion seemed to suddenly appear in my life. I hope this book will show how easily inclusion can be implemented, how worthwhile inclusion is, and to open hearts and minds to including all into our schools and communities.

As we began to gather these stories, it became apparent that although each family was unique, each child needed different support and help along the way, they all still had one thing in common – a desire and deep longing for their child to belong. They wanted to see their child fit in, find friends, and be part of a classroom, a school and a community.

As the parents of three sons we have had some truly fabulous teachers in our lives; sadly, we have also had some teachers that were not very good. In our experience, a wonderful educator is someone who is a life-long learner and is committed to continually learning from others, in addition to being a teacher.

Inclusion should happen in all aspects of life. We live in the year 2018—there is no reason to continue to segregate anyone. Special education classrooms should not be at the back of the school, nor should they be a dark and dismal place that highlights differences instead of how much we are all alike. Special education is a service, not a place. All students should have the ability to be included for some period of time in the regular classroom - with their typical peers. School is designed not only to educate, but to prepare us for real life and finding the way we each fit in. Have you ever seen a special needs line at the bank or at McDonalds? Schools should be a place where things are learned and practiced for real life skills. Let's teach compassion, empathy and patience and create a future where all of these students will grow up to work, play and live along side each other for the rest of their lives.

Inclusion brings to the surface a lot of emotions. It can be incredibly scary for the parents to ask, only to be told no. It is fearful to the expert teacher not to know how to teach a child with special needs. No one wants to fail the child.

Yet, inclusion, when done well, can make us all better human beings. The beauty of seeing friendships created, watching young minds grow and learning to show compassion should be an expectation for all students.

Inclusion is a value statement. Including a child indicates others see the value the individual brings, and they see the strengths and gifts that each and every child has. Let's concentrate on what a child can do, and what strengths they have instead of worrying about what they can't do.

We are all perfectly imperfect-and like a shell on the beach, each one has flaws and chips-yet they are still beautiful. Lets celebrate each other and the beauty and talents within each of us

Teachers, Educators, Administrators:
Come to the table and meet with us.
Come and meet my child.
See what gifts and talents he has.

It can be done!
It should be done.

My hope is that you will open your hearts and minds to including all!

Michelle Tetschner

Section 1: Stories to Share

A Diploma for Anna

Barbara Hoopes

I'm bursting with pride ... Anna is now a senior in high school and very close to earning a standard diploma—today she passed her Algebra Standards of Learning (SOL) test! It was her third attempt. She has worked so hard to understand all these concepts—a year's worth of math is a big chunk to take on in a single test!

Anna has passed all her History SOLs, as well as earth science. All that is left is reading/writing to complete her "verified credits," and we are looking at state-approved alternative assessments for these (e.g., Work Keys). The school has been very supportive and encouraging.

I can't say enough good things about the teachers and staff there and how Anna has been provided the same experience as every other student. It's not clear how much a standard diploma (vs. modified/applied studies) would matter to her future, but she has worked so hard to do well in school, it would be quite an accomplishment for her.

Recently we visited a university in Pennsylvania for a "shadow day." She attended two classes with current students, visited the dorm, and we had lunch in the dining hall. I really liked their program, and it seemed like a good fit for her. She's started working on the application, and we'll keep our fingers crossed!

Don't get me wrong. Our life is not all sunshine and roses—Anna is a true teenager: opinionated, moody, full of hormones (aka boy crazy), challenging our parenting abilities at almost every turn. Her executive function skills are still developing, but she rises to each challenge with determination and hard work. And every day she makes us laugh and is a source of pure joy in our lives.

All of this is to say... don't ever set your sights too low. Patiently keep trying things that are hard. Love and encourage. Most of all, allow your kids opportunities to surprise you, room to exceed your expectations. Because that will undoubtedly happen.

~~~~~~

Barbara Hoopes, is a mom/wife/professor. The younger of her two daughters has Down syndrome. She and her family live in Virginia.

#SinkOrSwim

Amy Alison

Let's say I want to learn to swim in high school. My parents are excited and also want me to learn to swim. The people who teach swimming have met me and see that I have Down syndrome. They think swimming will be hard for me. They decide it is in my best interests to take this slow and really assess the situation.

The first year they show me videos about swimming and review social stories about proper etiquette in a pool. Second year they take me to the pool deck and let me watch other kids swim for a few minutes at a time, as they do not want to overwhelm me. They let me practice swim strokes in my classroom but are not ready to put me in the pool. Third year they let me dangle my feet in the pool and get wet, but they are sure I'm still not ready to go all the way in the pool, as something could happen to me. I could flail around and drown or I may refuse to get out of the pool. Fourth year they start tracking my behaviors in the pool area because I get so excited. They decide I may do something unsafe, so they start limiting my pool deck time and determine I am still not ready for the responsibility of getting in the pool. Graduation comes, and I have not learned to swim. I go to a neighbor's house two weeks after graduation and while no one is looking, I jump off the diving board in the deep end and nearly drown. Thankfully, my observant neighbor rescues me!

Moral of the story: you have to get in the pool if you want to learn to swim. It may be scary but there is dignity in risk. I can never learn to swim if I don't have access to the pool and opportunities to practice swimming in a safe and supportive environment.

Let's talk about inclusion with gen ed peers. This scenario plays out over and over and over in schools all over the world. We cannot possibly put this kid with DS with his peers, as it might overwhelm him! He just isn't ready. He could do something unsafe. He can't

3

keep up with the other kids. We will have to take this very slowly. So we continue to segregate and isolate him. We "allow" him to visit a gen ed classroom infrequently during some of the most chaotic and unstructured times (recess, lunch, specials) and then wonder why he has behaviors while in there?!?! Then we literally throw him in the deep end of the real world post-graduation and he flounders, can't get or keep a job, loses his social network and may become isolated and depressed.

Research shows that lack of inclusive education leads to high unemployment, depression, and isolation in adulthood. We can to do better than this! We HAVE to do better than this. We need to be open to tossing a kid with DS in the deep end (gen ed) in a safe environment with supports so he can launch out post-graduation as a young adult with some real-world exposure under his belt. #sinkorswim

---

Amy Alison is the Chief Operating Officer of the Down Syndrome Guild of Greater Kansas City. She has been a strong advocate of inclusion for people with Down syndrome since 1995.

Inclusion for Anderson

Jillian Benfield

Earlier this year I felt a kind of panic well up inside of me that I had never experienced before. I was worried and anxious about my son Anderson's development. Anderson has Down syndrome. I knew Anderson was capable of walking, but he didn't want to. He hit a plateau with speech and occupational therapy was his least favorite. I had just completed six months of advocacy courses through Partners in Policymaking. I wrote an article on Inclusion that went viral and yet because I was a stay-at-home mom, it didn't dawn on me to start the inclusion process. He had only just turned two.

For three weeks, I dropped him off at pre-school and then went to my car and cried. I remember being sad dropping off my typically developing daughter at school for the first time, but this was different. I often say that parenting a child with Down syndrome is life intensified, the highs are higher, the lows are lower, and the angst that hung between the ignition and me was thick. But I kept taking him because of what happened on his first day. He walked at school. He kept walking at school even though he wouldn't do it at home. Inclusion was working. He was the only non-walker in his class and that was the motivation he needed to start taking his first steps.

Unfortunately, he could only stay at that school for three months because we were moving. So, I would drop him off at school and then research new preschools that would not only take him but wanted him. I found one. The director was genuinely excited to have their first child with Down syndrome. Anderson had been at his new school for two months when I approached his teacher about his development. She said, "He puts his head down when I try to get him to talk, but at circle time and lunch time, he starts 'talking' and answering questions."

Inclusion was working. It is working.

It's not only working for Anderson, but also for those around him. I told his teacher that I might be pulling him from school later this month because we are having our first IEP meeting at our neighborhood public school. She cried.

He's the only kid in his class who doesn't talk in sentences and has very few full words. Yet, words aren't needed to build a friendship. I linger around the gate to catch him laughing and hugging his friends. Us adults can provide Anderson the tools, but it's his peers who will motivate him to use them. Tomorrow we have our first IEP meeting. It's the first of many in our future and I can feel that thick angst hanging over me again.

I observed the classroom twice, Anderson will be the youngest, by far the smallest and the most behind. I thought about waiting. I thought about keeping him in his environment a little longer.

What if he's not ready?

But what if he is? I realized I couldn't be the one to stand in his way. Inclusion is how he took his first steps, and it will be how he continues to walk into a future that is his own.

Jillian Benfield is a military spouse and mom to three children, her middle child has DS. She writes at www.JilllianBenfield.com

Please don't Miss Her!

Linda Nargi

"I know who she is! She's the pink headphones girl!"

Ah, yes. The pink headphones girl. I hear you. You're talking about the headphones that help her cope with situations that make her feel overwhelmed. In addition to Down syndrome, she also has sensory processing disorder (SPD). I understand why the pink headphones may be the first thing you notice.

But please don't stop there. If you do, you will miss:

The girl who pays attention to everyone around her and notices when they are upset. She feels very deeply. Don't miss that.

The girl who loves to read and loves to learn. She is so very capable of learning. Don't miss that.

The girl who loves to sing. She may be a bit difficult to understand but she knows the lyrics to so many songs it will take you by surprise. Don't miss that.

The girl who loves to dance and has some serious moves. Don't miss that.

The girl who loves animals and loves to learn about animals. She probably knows more facts about animals and their characteristics than the average adult. Don't miss that.

The girl who loves to be around people—on her terms. She is easily overwhelmed, so it may be easy to dismiss her as not wanting to be involved or included. She craves interaction in small groups and one-on-one time with people. Don't miss that.

The girl who is tough as nails. Every week she sits still while her mama sticks two needles into her body so she can receive the immunoglobin therapy that she needs. She never complains. Despite everything she endures, she keeps a good attitude and is encouraging to others. Don't miss that.

Please don't miss her.

Linda Nargi is a wife and mom and a proud grandma. Her youngest two daughters have Down syndrome. She lives in Colorado and loves advocating for individuals with disabilities.

Advocating for Ellie

Lauren Ochalek

Our daughter, Ellie, will begin first grade next Tuesday and she could not be more excited. As the mother of a child with a disability, I would be lying if I said that I wasn't anxious about this new beginning, though, like Ellie, I too am excited to see where this upcoming school year will take her and her confidence in everything always brings me much peace.

Every school year has brought its fair share of new and exciting experiences for our girl, and it has always been humbling to look back and reflect on just how far she's come. After all, this was a baby whom doctors feared was incompatible with life.

To see her thriving is the joy of our lives, but I digress. Below are several pearls of wisdom from our family's first six years of walking along Ellie's educational path. While this advice is unique to our lived experiences, we hope that it may help others somewhere along the way.

Collaboration is Key...

We feel as though much of Ellie's educational success can be attributed to not only her intellect, drive, and beautiful disposition, but also the willingness of dedicated educators to see her potential and **presume competence**. From the very beginning, we have viewed Ellie's team, as we refer to them, as just that—a team. By Merriam-Webster's definition, a team is "a number of persons associated together in work or activity." In this case, the work at hand is the molding of our daughter into a confident, independent, and well-rounded individual who will someday be on her own (to the fullest extent possible) as a contributing member of society. Regardless of chromosome count, working with educators who see Ellie's worth has made all the difference and, for that, we are forever grateful.

We believe that a part of working as a team is both parties coming to the table and showing their hands long before the school year begins. As parents, coming to every meeting(be it an IEP meeting or parent-teacher conference)with thoughtful intentions and a vision statement can make all the difference in how the school year, and your child's educational journey in general, progresses. It helps immensely to set solid expectations and the tone for future meetings and communication. Discussing a child's strengths and weaknesses in an open, honest manner gives the team the benefit of understanding how your child best learns so that an individual plan for success can be formulated.

Optimism Along the Journey...

So much of Ellie's educational journey, we believe, can be directly attributed to a positive outlook and willingness to collaborate with educators. Going into a meeting about your child with "guns a-blazing" (as many parents of children with disabilities have been led to believe is necessary) is absolutely not constructive nor helpful to anybody involved. Instead, coming to every meeting with an optimistic, uplifting attitude and a willingness to work together is half the battle. Open lines of reciprocal communication are everything!

While it is critical to always be your child's best advocate, please know that, in general, the majority of educators truly do have your child's best interests at heart. It is time that we, within the disability community, no longer engage in fear-mongering associated with the education system wronging our children; instead we must embrace and support our educators and then, in the event that it is absolutely necessary, remind them of what the law states regarding FAPE and LRE as they relate to IDEA. Kindness and mutual respect make the world go round and can go a long way in fostering constructive relationships between home and school.

Gratitude and Thanksgiving...

As a family, we are very passionate about the work that our educators do to help our children every step of the way along their educational journey. We always make it a point to emphasize our appreciation for these (too often underappreciated) individuals who dedicate so much of their lives, both in and outside of the classroom, to the betterment of others. Teachers are responsible for helping to shape our future generations. The least we can do as parents is recognize them and show them our gratitude.

Final Thoughts...

We know that Ellie's educational journey may not always be all rainbows and butterflies (we also understand that our experiences may be very different from others), however, with a foundation built on mutual respect between parents and educators, we are certain that we'll always be able to put Ellie first in the collaborative decisions that are made to support her throughout the entirety of her schooling. We have been very fortunate, thus far, to have educators who believe in our girl: educators that consistently set the bar high while presuming Ellie's competence, a bar that Ellie is continually determined to not only reach but exceed. Ellie's journey, as a student who is fully included alongside her typically developing peers, has been the model and definition of positive inclusion in every way. Along with excelling academically, inclusion for Ellie has meant lessons in respect and appropriate behavior, while forming strong, beautiful friendships and positive self-esteem. I know, undoubtedly, that her typical peers have learned much from her also. Inclusion for Ellie and our family has been such a gift.

Our Vision for Ellie...

Below is our vision statement for Ellie and is shared with her educators at every IEP meeting and the beginning of every new school year:

"Ellie will lead a life as independent as possible with whatever supports in place that she may need to succeed. We wish for her to be valued, respected, and included throughout the entirety of her life. We expect that she be treated like any other individual and be held to the highest of standards. We plan on her earning a high school diploma and attending a post-secondary institution to further her education. It is our expectation that Ellie, as an adult, will have acquired the ability to work in a field that she desires and earn a livable wage; live independently, if she so chooses; and make a difference in her community and the lives of those around her.

With this vision in mind, we believe that the very foundation of the life in which Ellie is building will greatly impact her future; therefore, there is much value in the decisions that are made today."

Lauren Ochalek is a nurse educator turned stay-at-home mom, who, over the past six years, has worked tirelessly to advocate for Ellie and others within the DS community as a whole. Lauren has dedicated her time to various local and national Down syndrome organizations throughout the past six years, though her current involvement is focused on restructuring the Down Syndrome Connection of Anne Arundel County, an organization that is very near and dear to her heart.

Reading is Key

Jwanda Mast

Rachel is a good reader. She has always enjoyed reading and has won a lot of reading awards. She is very proud of the fact that she is a good reader. Rachel has good fluency and word recognition. She is a sight word reader. I jokingly say she has never seen a vowel she likes. This has seriously impacted her spelling, and spelling is not her strength. I had a party for myself the day we stopped having spelling tests at school.

Many children with Down syndrome are good readers. Many are like Rachel and have good fluency and word recognition. Like Rachel, they can read almost anything but do they understand it? Comprehension is the struggle. This is true for Rachel, too. With that I want to add a little disclaimer of sorts. Rachel can tell you about what she has read. She may not be able to tell you the answers to your questions about plot, writer's intentions, and so forth. We are okay with that.

From the time Rachel was small, we have put our eggs in the reading basket. Our theory has always been that reading is her ticket and window to the world. I would believe that whether she had Down syndrome or not. From before she was born we have been reading to her. We've been going to the library and she loves all types of books. At IEP meetings when they wanted to pull her out for extra help with reading, we said sure-but we want reading tutors too-we want both! Yep, that's right. We want the extra help and we don't want her pulled out during reading. We want reading immersion. When told we've never done it that way before, we told them it would be a lovely new adventure for all of us. We believe it has paid off. Reading has a social component and sometimes I think educators get a little too focused on academics. What do I mean by this? If Rachel is reading the same things as her peers, she can discuss

13

it in social settings. If she isn't reading the same things as her peers, she has two things against her. I saw this in action last year. They had read "My Louisiana Sky" in language arts. I drove a few girls home from school and they were talking about the book, the setting and the characters. Rachel chimed right in with everyone else. Had she not been in the class and reading it – she wouldn't have been able to participate in that conversation. They also read "The Outsiders" and worked on small groups. Her teacher even said that one day when asking the class questions, that Rachel had the correct answer to a question and she was right when the other kids were wrong! Rachel got them to understand and believe her! More skills for life!

I have completely digressed from the point of this blog. I wanted to share with you about Bookshare, Read Outloud and Read2Go. I hope that most of you already know but on the chance that you don't, I wanted to share a few fabulous resources.

Bookshare is a non-profit that helps you to get access to all kinds of electronic books including text books and it's free. You have to register and complete some paperwork including certifying that he person using the books has a disability. Our reading teachers weren't familiar with the program and they are now adopting it. The beauty of it is this is that it may take a little time but almost every book you may need is accessible and free. The Bookshare website tells you exactly what to do including how to download a free program (Read Outloud) for reading the books on your PC or MAC. The iPad app, Read2Go, has to be purchased but is affordable. The program reads the book to you phonetically and highlights as you read it. You can choose male or female readers and speed of reading. We slow Rachel's down because she tends to be a fast reader and this makes her focus on certain words. Rachel still likes to do her leisure reading (Dork Diaries, Diary of a Wimpy Kid, The Cupcake Diaries, American Girl books) on her Kindle on her iPad or by hard copy. However, she does read some of those on the Read2Go program on the iPad. They are using it in her Read 180 class and the teacher is able to help get the correct textbooks. We've been able to find the adaptive reader and all textbooks. It isn't perfect, we've had some issues with downloads to the iPad but figured it out. We believe over the long term, it will help with comprehension. There isn't any research to support this yet, but we think it can't hurt and Rachel likes it. I am not a Bookshare expert but I think it covers pretty much all grade levels, and I know some college students who are accessing their textbooks with this program. Be sure to share it with your teachers.

Jwanda Mast is a Disability Rights Advocate and mom to an amazing adult daughter with Down syndrome. She is the host of the disability themed blog called: TheSassySouthernGal

Annie: The Fight is Worth It

Theresa Stewart Mitchell

We had Annie's transition-to-high-school IEP this morning. I was prepared and feeling strong. I even brought food and tea!

But, I was not prepared when our current IEP junior high school team began the meeting by reading aloud a letter, telling the new high school representatives what it was like having Annie at their school for the last two years. There were three pages of testimonials from her teachers and administration!

Needless to say, I was bawling like a baby.

Here are a few quotes:

"Though our time with Annie has been short, the journey has indeed been a pleasure. Before we send Annie on her next adventure to high school, we'd like to share some of the experiences we have had."

"Annie is truly an angel..."

"Annie lights up when her friends greet her each day!"

"Annie's personality is very engaging..."

"Annie makes a significant impact on the lives of our students daily. I know she will be great at her next school."

"Annie is the type of student that every teacher should desire to teach. She has some academic and social challenges; however, her infectious spirit, stubbornness, sense of humor and resilience is magical."

"The...Magnet School will cherish our time for the rest of the school year with Annie and will miss the bright light that she shines every day, as she continues her journey in the land of high school."

These quotes are just the highlights. They told it like it is (the good and the rotten) so that her high school will be ready to support her.

I share this not to brag about my kid, because she has her challenges, lots of them. Instead, I write it to inspire younger parents to continue the fight for inclusion. It is worth it! Annie is very excited about HS. We have some work ahead of us because they have never included a child like ours. But, the team let me know this morning that the time and effort is well spent!

Theresa Stewart Mitchell lives in Rockledge, FL, with her husband and father of their two girls, one of whom happens to have DS. She is passionate about inclusion and advocates relentlessly in their community.

My Beautiful Johannah

Michele McGown

Johannah is my gorgeous, smart, fun, and witty 8-year-old daughter. My beautiful Johannah is fabulous and she lights up each and every room she walks into. People seek her out, any and everywhere we go. She also happens to ROCK Down syndrome like no other. Her life is full of love and she spreads it like pixie dust in a shimmering cloud around those in her presence.

Johannah is currently attending a public school in Oceanside, CA. This school has been loving and understanding to all of those who are differently abled. They even celebrate these differences with a "Differently Abled Day" at school. How cool is that?

The school as a community is teaching how important each person is in order to make a fully rounded society. The principal and staff work tirelessly to improve the education standard for those with different needs and their attempt for excellence is clear and identifiable. Johannah is invited to birthday parties, involved in performances, included on field trips, and treated as a TRUE STUDENT among her age-appropriate peers in her second-grade class. Her teachers expect her to work as hard and learn as much as any other child, yet they understand the approach to her ability to learn may need to come about in a different sort of way. Isn't that true for many typical children as well? The love for all of the differently-abled children is felt the minute you enter the campus. Our children aren't "different" there. They are just AWESOME CHILDREN. PERIOD.

Johannah's IEP experiences during her preschool years were nightmare, after nightmare, after nightmare. Everything was a fight and a struggle to accomplish. I held to my guns, as I know, as her mom, what is best for my child. I did not have pie-in-the-sky goals, but I did have obtainable ones I felt were necessary for her learning curve to improve her life. Those days are long gone. They did teach me to be stronger for JoJo. They taught me to not allow others to derail her life goals, but only to look for goals that will make her flourish.

When we moved up to kindergarten—Wow what a change! I sincerely have yet to meet a teacher that isn't excited to teach my daughter. IEP meetings are a group of minds that are working together to improve Johannah's learning experience. I feel like she is truly loved, respected, and challenged. The principle has attended every IEP. She is truly interested and vested in my daughter as a student in her school. She wants her to succeed the same as each of the students under her direction. She is a principle that takes pride in her school and students; it is more than just a job to her. You can feel this pride in each teacher, administrator, and aide throughout the school. The staff has a passion that is rarely seen. We work as a team with each other daily. We address and strategize with cohesive plans and modify them as needed. It is a wonderful back and forth meeting of the minds.

I say strive for no less, your child deserves it.

I have learned to be strong and be heard. I am always respectful, yet I never back down. I am willing to compromise when I feel it will fit, however am not a push over. Your child's future is at risk. Being an advocate for your child is imperative. Our children are just as critical to society as every other human being is. Our children deserve to be included.

Michele McGown is a wife and mother of two kids: their son Bayne and an eight-year-old daughter with DS. It's been an incredibly positive, loving journey!

Sharing the Victory!

Debra Docal

This is one of my favorite moments of true inclusion!

My son, Ory, is in the fourth grade at St. Louis Catholic School in Clarksville, Maryland. Ory (who has Down syndrome) is also a member of the St. Louis School boys' basketball team. The following is an email sent out by the coach to all of the team parents.

Enjoy~

"With Thanksgiving upon us, I thought I should share how thankful I was to have your sons on my team this past Sunday at practice. During a break in our scrimmage, we played a game of knock-out to work on high-pressure shooting. About half-way through the game, I heard the chants from the players who got knocked out grow louder and louder for Ory to win it. I was inspired by how, in such a competitive game where no one wants to wait a millisecond (or lose), that everyone following him waited patiently to get him his shot and that he hung in there with them. Everybody knew who the winner was (just like in a Rocky movie), so I blew the whistle to declare the victor and it was fun to see the hugs and high-fives and for everyone to share in the victory.

The fact that a game with one individual winner was made into an event where everybody won was not a coaching marvel, it was your kids. Thank them this week and appreciate how cool they are. And, also remember that they got that way because you are too. Happy Thanksgiving, Coach Ed Fatula"

Debra Docal and her husband live in Maryland with their son and three daughters. They believe an open door for students with special needs should part of every Catholic school's mission.

Inclusive education is about embracing all, making a commitment to do whatever it takes to provide each student in the community – and each citizen in a democracy – an inalienable right to belong, not to be excluded.

Inclusion assumes that living and learning together is a better way that benefits everyone, not just the children who are labeled as having a difference

(Falvry, Givner&Kim, what is an inclusive school?, 1995, p.8)

"Before we begin this IEP meeting, I just want to take a moment to tell you how **AMAZING** your child is. We're going to talk a lot today about all of the things your son can't do but I need you to know that he is so much more than the sum of his deficits. Your son has his own **PERSONALITY** with unique strengths and interests that make him such an **AWESOME LITTLE GUY.** If we had more time, I would love to sit down with you over a *cup of coffee* and chat about all of the precious moments I've shared with your son. But **TODAY IS ABOUT HELPING** him. So yes, we are going to *focus* on what he can't do, but that's only so we can make sure that he has *exactly the right* services to each his **FULL POTENTIAL** and shine through as the *amazing person* that you and I know him to be. **Are you ready to tackle this with me?"**

www.SpeechAndLanguageKids.com

Meet Abigail #Just Like You

Jennifer Whann-Bills

Meet Abigail, "Abby!"

She is 13 years old.

Abby loves all thing IT. She uses her Chromebook to create movies, to work on her photography, and do presentations for school. She loves movies and all things Disney. She also loves to sing and has her own karaoke machine. She knows thousands of songs and can hear a few notes or clips and know exactly what song it is and what movie it's from as well! She also loves hanging out with her twin sister, no matter what they are doing. She also loves to go on cruises.

She has adapted to having Down syndrome and what that means for her as a person and in life. She has overcome an educational system that wanted to exclude her. She simply said "No, it's not fair. Don't be mean to me" and walked right into class with everyone else. So we have supported that vision all the way through middle school, even taking on our county school district. She has changed every teacher and school she has attended, just by being herself and showing inclusion does work.

I see her as fearless, proud, deeply loving, and loyal. Quick to forgive. She has high self-esteem, but always encourages others. She also has CAS (childhood Apraxia of speech). So she has worked hard to be verbal and intelligible. She also loves to go to National Down Syndrome Society Buddy Walk on Washington and is a self-advocate. She's awesome because of who she is: sassy, funny, sarcastic, and intrusive. But mostly because she cares deeply and goes out of her way to ask how you are and make you feel better. She would be the first one to go hug the class bully if they were upset or tearful. She senses others' emotions deeply.

Abby, we love hearing that you are fearless and proud! You won't take no for an answer, and we love your fearless fight for what you know is right. Stay strong!

Abby is #JustLikeYou

Jennifer Whann-Bills is a wife, pediatric nurse, mother to twin girls age thirteen (one with DS). I love to advocate for individuals with disabilities and my present goal is for inclusion in the education system in middle school and high school. Continuing to speak to SEAC, VDOE, school boards, and local and national representatives.

Inclusion is the Human Dignity
That We All Deserve

David Long

"Inclusion is the human dignity that we all deserve."

"An inclusive school is where kids learn to care for each other."

"When you open your doors to children with special needs, you open your doors to the experts. They are the experts and they bring amazing resources with them. It lightens the load and enriches us all".

"When you take care of the social part of school, the lessons become easier."

"We are all here for one thing—to safeguard each other's dignity."

David Long is the vice principal at Our Lady of Lourdes Catholic School, Bethesda MD

From a Teacher:
Teaching from the Heart

Beth Greene

Sometimes we worry about the curriculum or standards-based testing and our lessons take a lot of tweaking and changing. Some lessons, the really good ones, come from the heart.

Raymond walked into my classroom a little shy and quiet. I was asked to go to a meeting at our school and my principal said a student with Down syndrome would be joining our school. My first reaction was more about me to be honest. Could I be the teacher he needed? How could I make sure his needs were met? How would I prepare the classroom? Very quickly I realized that I didn't need to worry about all of this. The lessons this year were from the heart. Raymond quickly, along with the rest of the students, settled right into 6th grade. Beautiful friendships were made, students helped each other, and they just came together as a group. I didn't need to worry, I just needed to open my heart and let my students lead the way. The year will go down in history as one of my favorites because I got to witness children all learning from each other and that included me. Our lessons were far from just the curriculum and the academic standards. They were learning to accept each other, that differences make us each beautiful, and that we are better together.

Beth Greene is a wife and mother from Scottsdale, AZ. She has been teaching for twenty-six years. She believes that teaching should always begin with the heart.

Brandon's Part in the World

Teresa Gruber

There are axis points in our lives when we go from teacher to pupil.

We learn that the true answers in our lives are not found in books or outside the walls of our home. They are found in the actions and deeds of our children. In my case, my son Brandon, on his own, has turned his Down syndrome into a platform to help others. He wants to help those who he says "are in need of hope because they are excluded in life."

It led me to conclude that when I grow up I want to be just like my son. Through my love and compassion, I want to teach others that no mountain is too high if we simply believe. His motto "choose kindness, work hard, and be yourself" is lived out loud every day of his life. I decided that it is my turn to do the same, so I am endeavoring to become what my son is: a leader and inspiration.

Once, while shopping, I engaged in a conversation with a salesperson. When I mentioned that I had a son with Down syndrome, her face changed immediately, taking on a look of pity that shouted out "Oh, I'm sorry!" She looked like a close family member had just passed away. But she provided the launching point for me to educate her on what she clearly didn't understand. She and others needed to know that my son is a vehicle that carries within him compassion, optimism, empathy, and caring far beyond the diagnosis. They need to know that my son is a person who has a clear vision and acts on his vision each and every day in spite of all the obstacles and roadblocks he encounters. He breaks barriers that you and I are not equipped to break. Brandon doesn't look at the "what if's," even if it sounds lofty to others.

One of my favorite stories is from when he was in middle school. Brandon was in the school play and had worked his way up to a supporting role! Mr. Schneider, the director, creatively had come up with the idea of assigning an understudy, just in case Brandon couldn't remember his lines. His choice for the understudy, Jim, was brilliant because Brandon knew him. Jim was an honor student, outstanding citizen, and he was also happened to be Brandon's best friend.

In the first of three performances, Brandon nailed all his lines, dances and was ready for the next two performances! He'd nailed it! Brandon was excited to perform, knowing a large part of the audience in attendance were his friends and were there to see him. Cue to the second performance and everything is going great. Suddenly, right before intermission, Brandon decides to go stage right after the song and doesn't return. We panic—where is he? where did he go? We can see the director dodge backstage to see what happened. Jim, his understudy, who was standing behind the curtain in place, was waiting for Brandon. He motions, "Where is he, oh my gosh?!" but it is time for action. Jim steps onto the stage to do the lines and finishes the part, saying the lines for Brandon. When Mr. Schneider went backstage to find Brandon, he calmly said, "You're on right now, did you forget?" Brandon shook his head no. Brandon said, "Oh that, I know, but Jim has been at all the practices. I had my chance, but he hasn't yet. I wanted him to be on stage to say my lines." With a lump in his throat and holding his tears back, Mr. Schneider said, "Let me get this straight, you did this on purpose and you wanted Jim to have a chance to be in the play?" Brandon nodded yes. "Now that he has, does this mean after the intermission, you'll finish off the rest of the play?" Brandon nodded yes again and said "I'm so happy for Jim!" Mr. Schneider shook his head, gave a fist bump, and said, "Rock on man!" Brandon had had a plan all along.

This moment left my husband and I with feelings of overwhelming pride. Once the initial "where the heck is he?!" feelings subsided, that is! Brandon's peers and Jim's mom thought Jim had covered for Brandon's mistake. It was then, I realized the pupil had become the teacher. My son had become the teacher. My husband and I were witnessing a transition that was completely unexpected. I knew then and there that I wanted to be more like Brandon. I was ready to allow those around me to have their moment to shine, if it was the right thing to do. Forget standard conventions, lead with your heart and include others in your journey! I left shaking my head and realized then that living like Brandon would not only enrich me but all those whom I touch.

Teresa Gruber is an advocate and mom to one boy, Brandon (22) with Down syndrome. They live in California and are co-leaders of Brandon's foundation, 321Life.com, which raises money to help underserved populations in their community

My Brother James

Aubrey Lambert

It was a wonderful experience. I had been praying a long time for a brother or sister and then one Christmas my parents told me: "Look at this picture. Who do you think this is?" I didn't know, and then they told me the most exciting news I had ever heard. We were going to have a baby! We went to the doctor and the baby was very healthy. Finally, the doctor asked if we would like to know if it was a boy or girl. I wanted a baby sister. My baby sister was going to look just like me. I pictured her riding next to me in the car, but it was a boy. At first I was a little bit sad, but then I became very happy.

Four months later James was born. I didn't know until I went to visit James that he had Down syndrome and he was deaf. I was very sad. I thought he wasn't going to be able to do anything or hear my voice. My parents said the doctors told them he wouldn't be able to walk, talk, sit up, or crawl for a very long time. One day, unexpectedly, I was sitting on the carpet with James and I propped him up against my legs. He sat up! I was so happy. Then he learned to roll over and later to stand up. James got a cochlear implant and now he can hear my voice! I realized no matter what people tell you, a baby with special needs can be amazing!

Some people think that children with special needs shouldn't be here. I think that they don't see how amazing people with special needs can be. They only see the outside, the way they walk, the way they speak, the way they do things, the way they look. People are scared because they think their baby won't fit in with the rest of the world. They think people will laugh at them or point at them in the crowd. They think they will be completely different. They are scared because they don't know about Down syndrome. When my parents told me that James had Down syndrome, I thought about all the things that people would see on the outside. I thought he would not able to run, play, speak to me, and would never be able to go with me to fun places. This wasn't true.

I discovered something wonderful. I discovered the inside, the kindness, the loving, the caring and everything good about James. I discovered that James can do many things, things that we cannot do. He can love much more than we can ever dream of loving someone. He sees the world in a way that I don't. He sees the world as a world of friends where everyone is kind and everyone is a big family. He looks up to me, my mom, and my dad like no one else would. All he has ever known is love. And that's all that he will ever give.

I think that when people find out that their baby has Down syndrome they should not be sad, they should be very happy. They should try to see the inside the way I now see my brother. Love your baby as I love my brother. There are many things in your baby that are very special. Your baby is incredible. He is a miracle and a gift from God. You should respect this precious gift. When you have this baby, you will have joy. Your baby will have joy. Your baby will love you, so I want you to love your baby back.

To tell you the truth, Down syndrome can sometimes be sad, but it can also be a wonderful thing. When I heard that James was deaf I felt like it was the end of the world for me, but when James got a cochlear implant I felt the happiest I ever felt in my life.

A baby with Down syndrome is worth respecting, worth knowing about, and someone you should love. I think that when Jesus talks about "the least of these" He is talking about these poor little innocent babies who want a chance at life. People may look at them as not worth loving, but God loves them the most because they are pure. They just love and that is the only thing they know how to do. We should be more like them. If we always loved, there would be no wars and no hatred. The world would be happy. Happy like a little baby.

Audrey Lambert is nine years old © 2017 Audrey Lambert. Published with permission.

"Expecting all children
the same age to learn
from the same material
is like expecting all children
the same age to wear
the same size clothing."
~ Madeline Hunter

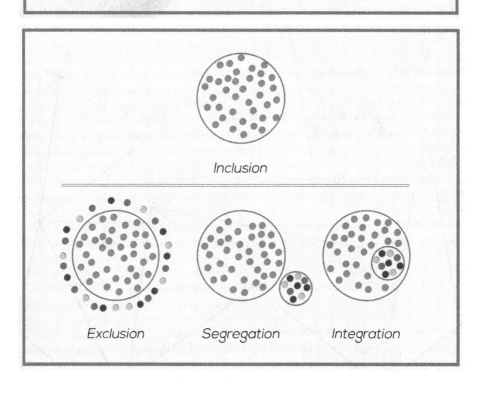

Inclusion

Exclusion   Segregation   Integration

Sean's love for music

Leslie Sieleni

When Sean was born back in 2000, we had no idea we were going to be joining this journey. You see, we did not find out that

Sean had Down syndrome until he was five days old. That's when life turned upside down for us. Not because we weren't happy with the birth of this beautiful child, but because of our fear of the unknown.

When it was time for my son to attend kindergarten, we were sought out in our community. They came to us before we even had a chance to look around at what other opportunities were out there. They suggested we attend a school that was not his home school, as the home school did not provide services for our son. The school was 4 miles from our home vs. his home school that was half a mile from our home.

At the time the kindergarten discussion was taking place, we trusted what was being offered to us would be the right option for him. We put our trust into the school and the educators. We believed what they told us: "this is the best program for your son and for his needs ... we offer great programing ... exactly what your son needs to be successful."

As the year progressed, we began questioning why he was not improving in his speech and vocabulary? Why was he becoming more and more frustrated and acting out? Why was he not advancing, but instead regressing from all the early intervention we had received beginning at three weeks of age?

The day I went to visit my son at school ... the light bulb went on! I walked into the segregated classroom/wing, where I saw my son eating a snack and watching a Disney movie with students who were non-verbal. That is when it hit me! THIS was why my son was not speaking. He was being educated alongside peers that were not verbal, either. Hello!!! We were told, "He is doing just fine for someone who is profound to severely disabled." What?! At that moment, we realized this was going to be a very intense educational adjustment for us!

So, we jumped in with both feet and have never stopped!!

Immediately we requested he be placed in the general education setting, alongside peers that he could learn from and they could learn from him. He would hear the language and exchanges between his friends. EVERY student including those who are non-verbal should be in this setting, not just my son. After one week of being in this inclusive environment, his vocabulary shot through the roof! His confidence also shot through the roof! He was so excited to be with his friends. Friends he saw out of school. Friends he got to have lunch with. Friends he played with every day! We finished elementary school with a very positive experience. He LOVED school and had so many friends.

We were happy that we advocated for inclusion so early on. We truly believed that all we had advocated for in elementary school would carry on throughout the remainder of his education in our district. We were so optimistic, but sadly mistaken. We had to start over. We toured the middle school only to find kids with special needs were still eating at a separate table. When we informed them that this setting would not work for my son, we were told by the principal that in order for my son to sit with his neurotypical peers at lunch, we would have to get a letter signed by the students' parents saying it was ok for my son to sit with them. What?! Of course, when questioned, they realized how silly that was and gave in. Sometimes it's hard to overcome what is the "norm" from years past and bring everyone to today's expectations and laws.

Class assignments came, and we did not agree with many suggested classes and signed my son up for the class he wanted to be in with his friends. He chose choir, science, language arts, and history, all with proper supports in place. Guess what—he ROCKED IT!

Always remember, you have the final say and you know your child best! He can and will learn, and he proved it! He came home and was so excited to tell me how the digestive system worked. He showed me where body parts were and even where his esophagus was located—even saying the word clear as day!

Our son has always been surrounded by music! He loves to sing and had been in the choir since elementary school. What music does for Sean is amazing. It is the core of his belonging. He has no fear and has such confidence when he is surrounded by music. He doesn't always sing on key, but he was the most enthusiastic singer I have ever met. In tenth grade, we were confronted with a teacher who didn't believe Sean should be in her class and made it clear to us all. She was fearful of having him in her class because she couldn't "fix" him. She was more concerned about perfection. Take the Regional Competition, for instance. This was a big day! The week before the competition took place, she reached out to me. She stated that we had made the agreement that Sean would not participate in the competition, as they are scored on musicality as well as formalities such as dress attire. I asked her to show me the documentation stating that we agreed he would not perform. She couldn't produce that document. I told her I would discuss with Sean whether he wanted to perform or not. His response was priceless! He told me to let her know that his classmates needed him at that competition! He was part of the team! He attended the competition with his classmates and to her surprise…they took home the highest mark!

We were so excited for twelfth grade! In high school, teachers treat each student like a young adult. Their expectations are much higher, and students thrive in this environment. We were so excited to be in the final stretch of his educational career. He was 100% mainstreamed with modifications to curriculum and support. Teachers were amazing and so excited to have Sean in their class. When it came to conference time, we realized that the advocating and educating of teachers was finally paying off!

Teachers came to us and thanked us for allowing Sean to be educated by them. Many said they had never had a child with a disability in their class, but because of Sean being in their class, they will now educate EVERY student differently. While this made us so incredibly happy, it was also so incredibly heartbreaking. Shouldn't EVERY student be given the same educational opportunity? We have come so far, yet we have so far to go! The federal law is too vague and holds no one accountable. Schools are doing what they believe is the law; however, I truly believe they are doing it backwards. Every student should begin their educational career in the general education setting with proper supports in place and modify placement if (and only if!) all avenues have been exhausted.

Sean has been truly blessed with great friendships and amazing opportunities all because of being educated in an inclusive environment. When students are educated alongside each other, they are changing the world as we have known it. It is time to end this vicious circle of segregation. As we know, inclusive education changes all students for the better. These peers are my son's future coworkers, boss, teachers, neighbors, and friends! These students have learned empathy, acceptance, and the value of EVERY individual. Yes, the road has been hard, but our son was worth the fight!

Leslie Sieleni is a mom to three, with her youngest having the attribute of Down syndrome. They live in Minnesota. They have fought hard for an inclusive life for their son and he is ROCKING IT!

Journey to Inclusion for Reese

Jennifer Dillon

When my daughter, Reese, was born with Down syndrome, one of the first things I promised myself, my husband, and Reese was that we would not treat her differently. We would take her home and create a plan that would allow our hopes and dreams for her to have a fully included life to not waiver. And that is exactly what we did.

When I returned to work, she went to daycare with typical kids. We went to mommy and me classes in our community with typical kids and families. As she grew older, we enrolled her in swimming, dance, and gymnastics classes with typical peers. When the time came for her to start elementary school, my plan for inclusion remained the same. The only thing that was different was that I knew if I was going to advocate for Reese to be educated in the same classroom as her typical peers, I was going to have to know my stuff.

I began the journey to immerse myself in the topic of inclusion. I read every word of the state and federal regulations, I attended workshops, and I became familiar with important terminology like "least restrictive environment" and "supplemental aids and services." The work paid off when our IEP meeting for kindergarten went relatively smoothly. The IEP team agreed with my request for a general education placement and Reese was enrolled at our neighborhood elementary school. I was elated!

However, kindergarten came with unexpected challenges. A kindergarten classroom is a busy place with a lot of kids, noise, and distractions. Reese struggled with behaviors and maintaining attention to tasks. In my weakest moments, I questioned if a general education classroom was the right place for Reese. Perhaps there were benefits to a smaller classroom environment where she would be with kids with similar learning needs. However, I knew in my heart that a special education classroom would not provide the same level of peer modeling and friendships that would prepare her for life. When I saw how she modeled the behaviors of her typical peers and accelerated in her learning and development, I knew inclusion was right and we needed to stay the course. Of course, it was going to be hard, but I was prepared for the challenge and in that moment I made the commitment to do whatever it would take.

Our IEP team met again and we began to look at what supports and services Reese needed to be successful in a general education environment. She was given a one-to-one aide and a behavior plan that incorporated a reward schedule and movement breaks. We ended kindergarten on a positive note. Reese had made a tremendous amount of progress over the school year. We were all so proud of her!

However, our situation was not perfect. As is the case in many school districts, ours was drastically understaffed and underfunded. The writing was on the wall—there would be hard-fought battles ahead in order to be a strong advocate for Reese if she was going to get the supports and services that she needed and deserved.

As luck would have it, Reese's father was offered a job that would move us to a state with a good reputation for disability services and education, and we jumped at the opportunity. While we knew that moving 1,400 miles to a new home would have challenges for Reese, as well as our entire family. Still, we arrived at our new home full of hope; however, our hope was short lived and the call to be a strong advocate continued. Reese was immediately placed in an integrated co-taught class at an elementary school within our district that was not our home school. We were told that each grade level had one integrated co-taught class and it was housed at whichever elementary school had the most students requiring a co-taught classroom. In addition, because students come and go, there was always a chance that the co-taught class would be moved to different schools from year-to-year. It simply broke my heart to think that Reese would not be able to attend the same school as her younger brother when he entered school. I went back on the advocacy train to prove that a special education program should follow the child rather than the child having to chase the program.

Still they had not thrown their best shot yet when only three days into the school year I was asked to come to the school for a meeting to discuss some challenges they were having with Reese. I expected we would share some strategies to help Reese adjust to her new environment and plan for our upcoming IEP meeting. Instead, I was introduced to another program that the district offers for students that require higher levels of support. When I asked about this programming, I was told that it was a self-contained classroom where Reese's only exposure to students without disabilities would be during lunch, recess, and specials. They had made this determination after only knowing my child for three days. I firmly, yet kindly, told them that I was not interested in their program and we agreed to adjourn until our regularly scheduled IEP meeting.

That next IEP meeting, and each of them for the next two years, was three hours long and focused on pages and pages of their documentation on what Reese could not do and never what she could. It was clear that the school did not feel Reese belonged in an integrated classroom, and the battle was all uphill to prove her worthiness to be educated alongside her typical peers. They continued adding more services and supports and cited her need for these services as further evidence for a self-contained placement. Reese's days were filled with data collection of her every behavior and movement. Instead of aides and paras helping her, they were documenting her days at the expense of her education and social development. She lost interest in learning and school and the stress took a toll on Reese and on our family. She became withdrawn and lost interest in activities that she used to enjoy, like ballet class. Her frustrations grew, and so her behaviors did too. She spent a large part of her day in the hallway refusing to re-enter the classroom. I saw the pain in my child's eyes and I thought about how it would feel to have my every move documented. How would it feel to go to a place every day where nobody believed I belonged? I knew that I could no longer send her to school. So, I made the difficult decision to homeschool her. It took our family a long time to heal from her experience at this school. Homeschooling had many benefits; however, I knew that there was a part of Reese that truly missed the social aspects of school.

As luck would have it, Reese's father was offered a fantastic job opportunity within the next two years. The thought of packing up our life again and moving was daunting; however, we welcomed the opportunity for change! I began researching the area and specifically researched school districts and their inclusion practices. I came across a school district website, and they shared my vision of inclusion. This time I enrolled Reese and her brother at our neighborhood school. Together! She was automatically placed in a general education classroom and assigned to a learning center for additional support, if necessary.

Reese now spends the majority of her day in a general education classroom. She receives some push-in special education services and some pull-out services in the learning center. Her general education teacher views Reese as a true member of her classroom. She emails me often to brainstorm ways to support Reese academically. Reese has developed friendships in both her general education class and the learning center. Her work is modified, and she receives accommodations to help her succeed. She is graded on her modified work, not on grade level expectations. She even made honor roll twice this year! Our IEP meetings are collaborative and I feel like I am a true member of the team. Our meetings are focused on Reese's strengths and how to support her academic and social development. Most importantly, Reese LOVES going to school again. She knows that she is part of the community and that she belongs.

Our journey to inclusion has been long, exhausting, and emotional. I have doubted myself on many occasions and wondered if inclusion is best for Reese. I've learned a lot about inclusion and how to advocate for Reese. I've had to look long and hard at my goals for Reese and my vision for her future.

Schools that value inclusion value the social development of their students just as much as they value the academic achievement of their students. Schools that practice inclusion look at each individual student's needs and do not make placement decisions based on diagnosis or classification. They start their IEP meetings with discussions about the supports and services that the student needs to be educated in the same classroom as their peers without disabilities, rather than beginning the discussion with why the student needs a self-contained placement. They recognize that all students learn differently and that all students need support to learn. Their IEPs are strengths based rather than deficit based. They don't sweat the small stuff when it comes to behavioral concerns and understand that sometimes less intervention is better.

Inclusion takes a village, but the benefits are well worth the effort! These schools are worth waiting for, worth searching for!

Jennifer Dillon is a mother of two children. Her daughter, Reese, has Down syndrome. She hopes her story will inspire others to continue advocating for school and community inclusion.

With Risk Comes Reward

Stacy Tetschner

Keeping fit, losing weight, following a budget—they are all difficult and they take discipline to be successful. Parenting also takes an equal, if not greater, commitment to ensuring we provide the best foundation possible for our kids to reach their full potential in life. With that commitment come trials, tribulations, risks, and amazing rewards. Having three boys, including one with Down syndrome, we made the same commitment to each of them: as parents we will work to provide the best possible foundation for them to achieve their goals to have a meaningful and rewarding life.

With our typical kids, it was easier because the systems in this world are set up to help them along their path. School, sports, socializing, and work all provide solid foundational tools. As parents we are still required to be actively involved in teaching and guiding them along the way. As we began navigating those same paths for our son with Down syndrome, we had a rude awakening. The systems we encountered were not always set up for him to reach his full potential; and in fact, many of these systems are set up to put him, and his differently-abled peers, into a predefined box with a predefined label leading to a predefined life. So, from the beginning of his educational planning, we knew the only way to show not only teachers, but the world, the value of our differently-abled children and adults was to ensure that they be fully included in the education process. Not only for him, but also for the other students who will be the world's doctors, lawyers, teachers, nurses, and parents, so they can blaze new trails of acceptance and inclusion.

Inclusion is not easy and there will be trials. For us, we've experienced the trials of bias and prejudice early on. We've had to confront a principal that was more concerned with overall school scores than the value of each student, and another that was committed to busing kids with "severe learning challenges" all to the same school across town so they would have their own system. There have been teachers that felt it was too hard to modify their lesson plans for those in the class that learned differently or needed some extra guidance, and we found they were committed to the system they learned and did not know how to vary from it. And yes, we have even been challenged by other parents for wanting our child included with their children.

With trials come tribulations. That translated to anger, tears, and questioning ourselves. It also meant seeing our child troubled, angry, and hurt. While these tribulations can exhaust us, they have also led to outcomes from others who have the influence we need and, in some cases, spur us to lead needed change. In what sounded like a wonderful plan, we took a risk and allowed our school district to move our son to what they called a blended classroom at a nearby school (not our neighborhood school) where half the kids in the classroom would be typical learners and half had learning disabilities and they were to learn together and from each other. In reality, the class split up into two classes every day, one with a teacher for the typical kids and one with a teacher for those with special needs. And even recess was split up for the two groups. We were naive and didn't think this was remotely a possibility when we agreed to it and when we requested to go back to our home school in a typical setting, the "district rules" didn't allow for that. We worked to make a change and hit a wall at every turn. Later in the week, I was in the yard talking to a new neighbor who had just moved in across the street and his kids had taken an interest in Raymond and wanted opportunities to come play with him. In the course of conversation, he asked how school was going for us, and I relayed our situation. He said he had some influence at the district level and wondered if it would be okay if he made a couple of calls to see if he could help out. A couple of hours later, he came back over, knocked on the door, and said he didn't have time to stay, but wanted us to know that our neighborhood school was expecting Raymond back at 9 a.m. Monday. Little did we know he was the immediate past school board president and a current state representative serving on the education committee. I asked how we could thank him, and he said get involved in leadership at the school board level—the inclusionary changes we wanted need leadership at the school board level from the parents that can champion the potential of our children.

We have taken that challenge not just at the public-school level, but even into private school. Raymond has been the first child with Down syndrome to be able to attend his Catholic elementary school and now a Catholic high school. When barriers for funding were thrown up, we held fundraisers and even started our own charity. It hasn't always been easy, not everyone has said yes along the way, and many times we were not sure we were going to get to yes. But the reward came not only for us but for everyone involved (principals, teachers, aides, parents, and, especially, students). The tide is turning, and we all have an opportunity to shape the future not just for our kids, but those that will come after them as well. Inclusion doesn't just happen, it's a discipline and, like anything in life that is worth pursuing, it takes commitment that will bring trials, tribulations, risks, and, especially, rewards. We have come a long way, but we are not across the finish line yet

Stacy Tetschner is father to three boys, one of whom happens to have Down syndrome, and who loves to say that Raymond is just like every other teenage boy—noise covered in dirt!

Swim Lessons and Ways to Include All

Blaire Hinks

Our Maggie was born with Down syndrome. She is ten years old and is currently mainstreamed at her school. She has five siblings and is slightly obsessed with movies, especially Disney movies.

In our part of town, there really isn't much offered when it comes to inclusive sports. Luckily, I have a pretty amazing village that has done nothing but open doors for my daughter!

Our first story of inclusion started when Maggie was just a baby. We started her in swim lessons at three months old. She was always with typical kids in every class she attended. As she got older, things never changed and neither did the teachers' expectation of what she can do. She loved swimming and loved making friends! We all knew that Maggie learns better in a physical environment where she can mimic her typical peers. There was never any room for frustration because the teacher accommodated accordingly without singling her out. She swam races with her peers and had contests to see who could get the most rings from the bottom of the pool. She was always impressive with the ring diving exercise since she was rather good at sinking! The other kids would always comment at how fast she was at getting to the bottom. The typical kids in her class knew that she was a wee bit different, but due to the attitude of acceptance that was being shown by the staff, they never thought twice about it. They cheered her on when she was doing well and offered to help when she needed a boost. Swimming, for Maggie, built confidence in herself. It will be a life-long love for her!

Our second story of inclusion involves a coach that was willing to have her on his t-ball team. This league typically doesn't have children with disabilities. Maggie's coach brought her on and treated her like any other child, though it was his first time coaching a child with special needs. We had a friend that assisted during games to make sure she was going to the right base when she was supposed to, and she practiced like the rest of the kids, completing all the activities right next to her typical peers. The coach created an immediately inclusive environment when he invited Maggie on his team. He never once allowed for any type of negativity towards Maggie and encouraged the players to help when they saw that it was needed and to encourage ALL their teammates. Maggie soared during the three seasons she played for this coach. She loved the team atmosphere. She would cheer for a teammate when they were up to bat and give them a pat on the back when they crossed the home plate. To this day, she loves to play catch with her brothers in the backyard.

Blaire Hinks is mom to six kids; Maggie is the second oldest. They love Arizona and love meeting new friends.

Food Court

Janet Romo

A group of moms who each have a teen with Down syndrome all decided to meet at the food court of our local mall to give our kids a chance to hang out together socially. One of the teens decided he wanted to get more soda. My daughter, Lily, and her friend Josie watched with admiration as Jacob handled the whole process on his own. Lily is quite shy and so doing this on her own had not been something she had tried or even shown interest in yet. But after seeing Jacob seamlessly order his drink, both Lily and Josie decided that they wanted to go to the counter and order water by themselves. I told them to go ahead. They walked confidently up to the counter at McDonald's. The high school kid working the cash register asked the girls what they would like. Lily and Josie fell silent. Even though both were perfectly capable of saying they wanted water, they were too nervous. They just stared at him.

The cashier didn't miss a beat. When he got no response from the girls, he asked them if they would like something to eat. They both nodded their heads no. So he asked them if they wanted something to drink. This time they both shook their heads yes. He asked if they wanted soda. They shook their heads no. He then asked them if they wanted water. They nodded yes. He went over and grabbed them each a water. Both girls were giggling and on cloud nine walking back to the table with their waters. They were so proud of themselves. What was so remarkable about this was that the young man knew how to question them and he was not put off by their awkward silence.

I had been standing in the background in case they needed me, but it turned out they could do it without my help. I walked up to the young man working at McDonald's and told him that he had done a wonderful job helping the girls place their order. His response made my heart so happy! He said that when he was in elementary school, he had some kids like them in his class.

I realized that I had experienced the uncalculated side effect of inclusion that might make the biggest impact on kids with disabilities: the impact that it makes on the gen ed peers!

Inclusion made it possible for two shy teens with Down syndrome to successfully order at a food-court restaurant without help from a parent or another adult. This young person who helped them had been trained organically through inclusion.

Inclusion prepares general education students for a diverse world, a world where many different people live and work.

Janet Giel-Romo Ed.D. is Lily's mother. She writes Austin & Lily curriculum for students with an intellectual disability (ID). Her passion is developing students with an ID to their potential.

Fletcher's Love of Theatre

Karen Jones

For many of us, we never thought what inclusion meant or looked like until we had a child with special needs. For the most part during the past eighteen years with our son, Fletcher Jones, born with Down syndrome, we have been blessed with wonderful programs with teachers who openly welcomed him. We have also had "those moments" that he was not welcomed or was told this would not be the best place for him, including a kindergarten religious education program at our church. As much as it hurts, it is also a blessing to know that our son would not be welcomed.

One of the most valuable and painful lessons for parents to learn is inclusion only works if everyone is on board! Up until the summer of 2016, Fletcher was born and raised in downtown Chicago. From three months old, Fletcher received early intervention therapy at home and attended a program for typically developing children at the Chicago Park District. He also attended a weekly music program, again for typically developing birth to three-year-olds. The music teacher actually wrote a song about him entitled "Fletcher!" Fletcher participated in the same programs as his older brother (by twenty-two months) had attended.

At three years old, Fletcher began Early Childhood Special Education with the Chicago Public Schools system. Since our neighborhood public school did not offer these classes, we researched a dozen programs and decided on a class about twenty minutes north of our home. With an amazing and innovative teacher, Fletcher would attend afternoon classes daily with a class size no larger than ten students. At the same time, three mornings per week, Fletcher also attended "Kiddie Kollege" another Chicago Park District preschool program for typically-developing students from 3–5 years of age.

This was a total-inclusion class without the need for any aide or paraprofessional. Life was good and busy!

Fletcher began kindergarten at five years old and transferred back to our neighborhood public school where his brother was also attending. Fletcher was in a fully-inclusive class and thrived. As there were other special needs students in the same class, an aide was present in the room, but Fletcher never required a one-to-one aide. Fletcher appeared in school musicals and talent shows throughout his time at Ogden elementary. Fletcher was the school mascot, the Ogden Owl, for two years and continued appearing onstage in the school's musicals. He attended there through his sophomore year.

In the summer of 2016, our family moved to Chandler, Arizona. Fletcher came from a high school of 400 students to one with over 3,600 and growing. Since beginning Perry High School in Gilbert, Arizona, Fletcher has found his home within the talented Perry Theater Department. From the first home football game where the Drama Club was painting Puma faces for fundraising, Fletcher has been warmly welcomed to this program. In his first year, Fletcher appeared on the Perry Stage in Senior One-Act plays and a small production of *Blues*. That year Fletcher even had enough volunteer hours and stage time to earn his way into the Perry Thespian Society at the end of the school year! When his name was announced at the ceremonies, the loud applause of his classmates along with their parents was amazing.

After an award-winning year for Perry's production of *Mary Poppins*, the director decided to put on *White Christmas* in December 2017. Auditions were held in early October. The cast list was posted, and Fletcher's name appeared in the ensemble cast and he had lines along with dance numbers. He appeared several times throughout the show and did his lines with style and drama.

Again, inclusion is successful when everyone is on board to ensure that it is the best place for the student with special needs. We have been very fortunate to have directors and teachers who wanted not only the best for our son, but also to be fair to their programs. Drama has been an easy way to inclusion for us, and we are grateful to Perry High for being open and willing to help Fletcher find his place there.

Karen Jones is blessed to be called Mom by her two fun-loving sons, Douglas and Fletcher. She, along with her husband Briand, and sons, live in Arizona. Life Is Good!

Wrestle for Inclusion, Karsten!

Wendy Brunner

The school year did not start well. We were returning to the school district where Karsten, my now fifteen-year-old son, had spent most of his academic career. Hopes were high, based on word-of-mouth that the high school program was terrific, and that the teacher was fantastic. But, two weeks before the start of school, the fantastic teacher quit. It was August and school was starting, so we stuck to the plan thinking it would work itself out.

Fast forward to October. We were experiencing a severe lack of inclusion and every day my heart was breaking for my son. It turns out that Special Ed teachers were hard to come by in a small school district. The ones we had were temporary and demonstrated a pronounced lack of understanding, motivation, and, for some, even a sense of right versus wrong. We had parent meetings, met with the principal and with the district, yet our kids continued every day to receive far less than they had a right to, deserved, or most importantly were capable of. When I would walk Karsten into his bleak classroom, he knew his routine, which was to put his backpack away and go sit at the table and play with Legos. There was no sign of homework or learning. I know there were plenty of movies and lots of Legos.

What does it feel like to know your child is not being given a chance? It takes your breath away. It is a punch in the gut. I felt like I felt when I was ten years old and Gary Taylor punched me in the stomach. Maybe it wasn't what he intended. Maybe he didn't mean it. But it hurt. Real bad.

So, here's the good part of the story, though it is still new and evolving. I guess I would say that wrestling saved us. I thought Karsten would be good at wrestling, so I talked to the principal and the coach. The coach was on board without even a hint of doubt. He jumped in with both feet. And he knew his guys, and that they wouldn't bat an eye either. I was nervous though. This was the first team Karsten would be on that was not geared towards special needs. He was on his own. With the big guys. After the first practice, here comes Karsten out of the wrestling room door with his shirt off and strutting his stuff. I had to chuckle. Who was this? I noticed a few of the other guys (the ones who had clearly visited the weight room) without their shirts on, and Karsten had his copycat eye on them too. Peers! I had a fluttering of excitement that this was the right thing.

Wrestling is hard. I never knew. The coach works them like they are at boot camp. I peeked in on a few practices and Karsten was participating, with breaks. And at the end of every practice he would come out just a little bit taller, just a little more confident, and proud of himself. Right before my eyes! We went to our first meet, and Coach arranged for a wrestler from another school to take on Karsten in a "real" match, in front of the crowd of hundreds of people. Now that's a coach!

Karsten was visibly nervous. He didn't push too hard, but the other boy just stayed with him. Eventually, Karsten kicked it in a little, and though I was focused on him, I could sense what was happening in the gym. There were two other matches going on at the same time, but slowly, section by section, people started to pay attention to what was happening on Mat One. I could hear them start cheering my boy on. I could tell they were all rooting for him. When Karsten pinned his opponent and the referee raised his hand in victory, the whole gym erupted in cheers. And I, of course, erupted in tears.

The tears were only partially for Karsten and his inclusion in this event. They were also partially for me, because I never thought I would have the experience of cheering my son on at a high school wrestling match. Something so normal. I felt included.

But my tears were also for the feeling that spread around that gym. There was love. There was happiness. There was joy in watching the success of another human being. It didn't matter that the match wasn't real. To Karsten it was one hundred percent real and no one would disagree. They cheered for him just like they did for the state champion. After winter break, we got another new teacher. This time, it was the teacher the parents had been requesting all along. She is young, vibrant, kind, and ready to expect the best from our kids, to push them to learn the skills they will need to lead a good life.

Karsten isn't included as much as he could be, but we're working on that. And every time my boy participates as an equal—one with different abilities—there is a tiny revolution in how others think and feel about those with special needs. I have witnessed it and know for sure: the more the better (for all).

Wendy Brunner is a writer and mom of two including a Down syndrome teenager who promotes the global view of Down syndrome at DownSyndromeEverywhere.com #RevolutionOfTheHeart

We Made Inclusion Our Norm

Stephanie Mefford

How excited we were after being married for sixteen years when we found out I was going to have a baby! My husband, Dan, was speechless as I told him the news. He made me take a home pregnancy test after I already told him one test was positive. When we went to the doctor for my first checkup, he made me take another— he was that excited! We serve on staff at our church and the whole congregation was glad to hear our news. At our first ultrasound, the doctor thought the baby might have fluid around her heart. Our entire church all diligently prayed for her health and well-being. We welcomed a baby girl and named her Dana after my husband. We also wanted her to have a short name, in the event she did have Down syndrome. Not only did she have DS, but she was born with transient leukemia. Fortunately, Dana's leukemia resolved on its own without treatment. Those days of waiting and multiple blood draws were anxious ones but were soon put behind us as we entered a world of early intervention therapies. Dana had weekly visits from a physical therapist, occupational therapist, and speech therapist.

Everything we learned from the Down Syndrome Guild of KC led us to consider possibilities, not just limitations. Soon it was time for our daughter to attend early-childhood education, beginning at age three. Dana was placed in a classroom with eight children with Individualized Education Plans, two peer role models, a special education teacher and a paraprofessional. When Dana graduated preschool and entered kindergarten, we advocated for inclusive education with a minimum of pull-out instruction time with a full-time paraprofessional.

I noticed early on that Dana learned a lot from other children and since she did not have any siblings, being around other children in the school setting was important.

IEP meetings were difficult over the years. We have had advocates attend in person and by phone. At times, I had to knock Dana's goals down to almost nothing because the school team was so concerned she would not be able to make much progress in the general education setting. I kept on teaching at home, finding out what assignments were being given by talking to other students. Sometimes it takes a village! And I was lucky enough to have friends who would share their children's graded work, which they kept for me to see and review.

Inclusion is not the norm in our area, so we made it our own norm.

As I considered Dana's middle-school placement, I knew first of all I did not want her in "Life Skills" classes learning to dust library shelves and do laundry. We teach her those things at home! I am happy to say that in seventh grade Dana is included most the school day (96%) with her general education peers. She has three classes of co-teaching (reading, writing, and math) and no paraprofessional. We work a lot on homework. I buy school textbooks that I learn about on back-to-school nights or school preview tours. I am grateful this year's teachers have been more forthcoming about what reading assignments she will have in the following week, which allows us to have a chance to review them as our weekend schedule allows and preload that material as much as we can.

She has ambitious IEP goals involving solving math equations and writing paragraphs. Over the winter break, all on her own, Dana wrote out 7 sticky notes with terms such as nucleus, cell membrane, prokaryotic, eukaryotic, DNA, and RNA! She even knew many of the definitions. She continues to amaze us. She even took violin last year in school and this year even tried the cello.

Dana is a part of the community in which we reside. We go to opening receptions at the local art gallery, movies, the park, local swimming pools, bowling, and more. Our church family is very accepting of Dana and holds her to high standards, just like any other child. I am so proud of her and her desire to learn. She loves being a teenager, especially since it means getting to sleep in on weekends. She loves to say, "Teenagers need their sleep, Mom."

Stephanie Mefford is often referred to as "Dana's mom." She and her husband Dan live in Virginia. Stephanie enjoys reading for pleasure and visiting with older adults in her church.

Brady's Friends Overcome

Tena Green

I have always been a huge supporter of inclusive community and education. I believe that the community needs to be comfortable with my son Brady, as well as Brady being comfortable in the community. When Brady was just six weeks old we found out that he indeed was born with an extra chromosome, also known as Down syndrome. I was twenty-six years old when Brady was born and I did not think it was possible for me to have a child born with Down syndrome (I mean after all, only 'old' mothers have children with Down syndrome). Once we got the diagnosis, we were given this wonderful book about what to expect. This book told us things like our son was probably not going to talk, drive, have thyroid problems, basically a whole list of NOTS! I remember being in tears looking at my husband and saying, I would never read a book full of things that say what my child cannot do. So I threw that book in the trash!

Brady started preschool and attended a school with twenty-six other four-year-olds. He had a great time and thrived. He started Kindergarten with his friends. Through his elementary journey he continued to make friends, thrive, and learn.

Then in fifth grade we had to do a transition meeting with his IEP team and the team at the middle school. We were really looking forward to middle school, until we realized that the transition team that the school wanted us to meet with was a different middle school then what his friends were attending. You see in our district, you can 'choice' into any school you choose. This means you can pick a school, fill out an application, and wait patiently to see if you get accepted (if you live in the zone of the school, you do not need to fill out an application). Our school district also offers 'site-based services,' which means based on your child's IEP the school filters them to a certain school. We have been told that this is a fiscally responsible thing for the school to do. I can get behind the fiscal responsibility stuff but, what I could NOT get behind is that the middle school they wanted to send my son to was NOT the same middle school that my son's elementary feeds into, meaning that Brady would not be attending middle school with his peers.

Naturally, I had a meeting with the district to see if they could help me with this. They said that we had to fill out a school of choice application and only if the middle school would accept him could he could go there. I sat down at the computer excited to fill out his application, and the first thing they asked for was his student ID. I typed in his student ID and, voila, the application automatically populated his name, parents' names, address, etc. It also automatically checked a box that said he had an IEP. Right away my heart sank! I tried to uncheck that box, but I could not. I knew that if the school only had an IEP to read that they would not know my true son. The boy who can make you laugh, who brightens your day when you see him, and, most importantly, the boy who is a great friend. I could not send that application without meeting with the principal. I wanted to paint a true picture of my son. I did a short video of a handful of Brady's friends. I asked them, "Why do they want Brady to be in their school next year?" His friends said things like "because he makes school fun," "because he is my best friend," "because he taught me that just because you have a disability doesn't mean you do not have a lot to learn."

My husband and I met with the principal and showed him the awesome video of Brady's friends. The principal had tears in his eyes and told us that he was sorry, but he could not help us. You see because our son had an IEP, the district had him slotted to go to a different middle school. As you can imagine, by now my head is spinning. When students transfer from elementary to middle school, most of them care only about transitioning with their friends. I looked at my husband and said we need to get Brady's friends to speak at the school board meeting. This was a Friday. I checked the schedule, and there was a meeting on the next Tuesday. I immediately started texting Brady's friends' parents to see if they were available on Tuesday to speak at the school board meeting. One by one they said yes. My heart was so full of compassion and gratitude!

Tuesday night we had such a big crowd that wanted to speak that the board gave us ten minutes total to speak, instead of the normal three minutes per person. My husband and I both had a three-minute speech planned; however, we both knew that having Brady's friends speak would mean more than us speaking. His friends got up in front of a room full of adults and talked about social injustice and why it is important that Brady is able to go to middle school with them. By the time our ten minutes were up, it was obvious that Brady and his friends changed the mind-set of that whole room.

By Friday, the principal at the middle school we wanted Brady to attend called us and said that Brady could attend school there. We are happy to report that that was two years ago and Brady is loving school!

You can watch his friends speaking up for Brady here: https://www.youtube.com/watch?v=ZygpUe_m_G0.

Tena Green who is a mom to three wonderful boys, the oldest of whom has Down syndrome. They live in Colorado and love the beautiful mountains.

Our Anna: Looking Past a Diagnosis

Dawn Sikes

When we received the post-birth diagnosis of Down syndrome, I didn't know up from down. I only knew that every dream I had for my only daughter was over. Out the window and nothing I could do to change it. Well, little did I know that my response to her could and would change it all.

I wanted Anna to be happy and full of life. I had hopes she would want to cheer, play softball, do pageants, have friends, have a boyfriend, go to college, and someday marry. You know, all the things a parent hopes for.

For the first three weeks I was all over the place. An emotional wreck. Then we saw a doctor, a geneticist, and he changed our life. He told us to trust her just like we had done with the older boys! NO DIFFERENT. He told us to expect her to do the things the boys did and to not let her diagnosis alter those expectations! We left there with a vision that I cannot put into words!

She entered kindergarten and actually did two years of kindergarten because she did so well under the teacher. These are where the fundamentals are built, and I wanted her to get the best foundation possible. Anna has always been fully included. She attends all mainstream classes with her typical peers. Her teachers see her accomplishments and they encourage her. They fully support her even though it's probably more challenging to find the appropriate accommodation for her tests. The teachers hold her to the same expectations as other students; she may need a little extra time, but still the same expectations. This is inclusion at its best!

Anna met a very good friend in elementary school, and she has been one of the very best things in her life. Jade never saw difference in Anna and she made sure others did not either.

Anna is now a junior in high school. She cheers and she does pageants! And very well, I might add! She is a volunteer at a local hospice in her home town. She is the first student with DS at her high school to become a member of the National Beta Club. Last spring the softball coach asked Anna to be a part of the team because she saw how much Anna loved being a team member. She knew how much Anna loved to be a part of the "group." She saw inclusion and never thought twice!

Anna is blessed with an amazing school! She has teachers who look past her diagnosis and see her ability! They see that inclusion has helped Anna grow into a confident, smart, caring, loyal young lady!

Dawn Sikes is mom to four children: three boys and one girl. They live in a small town in Alabama. They feel very blessed.

Missing Christian

Kelsey Sprowell

My little brother died last month, nine days before Christmas and three days after being admitted to the hospital with pneumonia. He was 24 years old.

Christian loved being outside, playing guitar, going for walks and people-watching. He ate chips and salsa almost every day and actually enjoyed helping with chores around the yard. He loved swimming, riding his horse during hippotherapy appointments, and being in church, especially on Christmas Eve.

Like most older sisters, I have a trove of stories to tell about growing up together. I'm the oldest of the four of us, the bossy one, whereas Christian spent his whole life as the baby of the family - the unfortunate consequence of being born last. His first words were "stop it" and "let go". For most of his childhood, even the dog was bigger than he was. When I was 15 and Christian was seven, Grandma came to town and wanted to teach me how to drive; when she and I switched seats and I put the car in gear, Christian started to cry from the back seat.

He loved the snow and wearing his snow pants; he'd yell "PANTS!" whenever he put them on. After college, when I started a job as a ski instructor, our sister Courtney told him that I got to wear my PANTS every day, and he looked at her incredulously and said "What?!"

Christian was born with Down syndrome and Fragile X Syndrome, both inherited intellectual developmental disabilities. Not that it would have changed anything, but my parents weren't aware of either of these labels before he arrived. His diagnoses simultaneously changed our family life drastically and was just part of who we were. I grew up much more quickly than my peers because of exposure to my parents' grief, and yet (to their endless credit) they raised us to work hard, together, resisting any feelings of pity or pride for our circumstances. Despite his disabilities, and thanks solely to the will of my parents,

Christian was fully included in typical classrooms throughout his education. He was also subject to his peer culture; he sagged his pants, listened to the same music as other kids his age, and would have gone to prom if he'd shown the slightest interest.

He was way better at basketball than I'll ever be.

Christian was non-verbal -in my opinion, by choice. He could say plenty of things; he just didn't need to. He only spoke when it improved the situation. One time a couple of years ago, Andrew and I were home in Fort Collins, having pizza at the kitchen table. Andrew cracked a Bud Light and Christian pointed to it, so Dad got him a beer, too. He picked it up and chugged half the can like a college freshman. When he set it down, he looked at Dad and said "hot!" — an apt descriptor for the burn of a chugged beer. Once he got in trouble for yelling "Fu**!" at a staff member who made him turn down the music he was listening to (a Kanye West album I'd ripped for him -a particular point of pride for me). Words have power. He knew that they had more power when he used them sparingly.

The most noticeable facet of his disabilities was an impulsive behavioral disorder wherein Christian would grab whoever was nearest to him. It came on quickly and intensely and, so long as someone near him could deescalate the situation (which our family and his care providers were trained to do), passed quickly, too. It was frightening for people who didn't know what was going on, but Christian couldn't control it any more than someone having a seizure can control their own brain activity, and what scared most people didn't scare us. He hated when it happened; if it was especially bad, he'd cry and apologize. To help him feel relaxed in group settings — to relieve any anxiety that he might accidentally hurt someone — Christian often wore oven mitts on his hands in public. Because of this, I worried that people would think he was "more disabled" than he was, and I wondered if it ever embarrassed him. For what it was worth, he didn't seem to mind.

The day Christian died, all seven of us were together in his hospital room. He lied in bed with my mom snuggled up next to him; I sat at his feet, with everyone else in chairs around us. We prayed the Lord's prayer and Christian reached out to hold my hand. Mom washed his face with a cool cloth; we sang Silent Night together in the dark. It was quiet and peaceful when he took his last breath. After he passed, I kissed his face and breathed in the scent of his skin, wanting to hold onto him for as long as possible.

The following weeks, including his funeral on my birthday, were the worst of our lives. But we were together. Friends of my parents dropped off casseroles, paper plates, and FIVE hams (five!). Collectively we received hundreds of cards, notes, posts, texts and calls, from an unimaginably broad group of people, all of which buoyed us through deep grief. We cried a lot and slept only a little. And in the middle of it all, the damn internet quit working. It was completely erratic — it went in and out for days. When it came back, although it should have remembered the network, all of our phones and computers required us to input the wifi password — The Red Sox Are In Town — the "heads up" keyword we used when Christian was having a bad day and might grab you. Comcast came out to check the wiring; Dad spent $300 on a new router & modem. Nothing fixed it. None of our devices malfunctioned at the same time, and the internet had never behaved that way before. It stopped when we all went home; we realized afterwards that it was Christian. Mom said: "If you're gonna get this group's attention, that's a brilliant approach."

Donations made in Christian's name to the charities we designated in his obituary have totaled more than $5,000 (and counting), a sign of the impact he had on the people who knew and loved him. I wonder, too, if this outpouring is a response to our friends' shock that a vibrant kid could fall ill and die so easily. My parents have always said that of the four of us, Christian would have been the All-American, were it not for his disabilities; his biology cheated him out of what could have been an incredibly successful, active, productive life. It's been said that "the depth of your grief is equal to the depth of your love," and for us, it's equal to the depth of our anger at what he missed out on, too.

Calling things 'retarded' was de rigueur when Christian was born. I had a particular knee-jerk reaction to hearing it: when someone used that word around me, I corrected and lectured them. I was unapologetic and mean to literally anyone, friends and strangers alike, who did it. My mom talks about having to pull me aside in Target and teach me about boundaries, about not correcting people we didn't know, but I did not — and still do not — subscribe to that belief. I have a particularly strong memory of being at a college football game when someone nearby called something retarded; one of my best friends looked at the guy and said "Oh you've done it now" before I launched into him. Use that word near me and you get publicly shamed, full stop. It's part and parcel of a fear I had of people painting Christian with a broad brush. He was so interesting and funny and smart and introspective, and reducing him to 'retarded' made me viscerally angry. I feared that people would see him as a disability, that — due to no fault of his own — he'd start from 10 points back with every person he met. Many able-bodied people are inclined to assume that people with disabilities aren't capable of anything, or that they should be treated with pity, or both. Christian had a lot of courage and patience; he never let other people's judgment get to him. He was also fantastic at ignoring it.

Having a brother with a disability is an experience that only people who have siblings with disabilities can understand. From an early age I felt profound grief for Christian -and because of Christian — but also fierce love. I would have done anything for him. I knew what he would never be capable of, and it broke my heart to think that he might be aware of it, too. I mourned the typical brother I'd missed out on, but out of respect for Christian, and to protect him, I hid these feelings from everyone. I held onto a host of fears for Christian's life — at first, that he'd never learn to drive, that he'd never get married; later, that he'd get cancer or multiple sclerosis and wallow in a hospital bed, that an overeager police officer would misinterpret an aggressive episode and shoot him. I was afraid of what our common future looked like in the age of a president bent on eliminating funding for the programs that gave Christian's life richness. I worried about what it would be like for my husband and children someday, after my parents were gone, when decisions about Christian's care fell to me. I'm still afraid that people will think that his death isn't as tragic as if a typical 24-year-old had died, that it's sad but acceptable when people with disabilities die young. It's not.

More than once, I had to choose between living close to Christian and being in his life, or moving away and giving that up. He dictated two of my major life decisions: I stayed in Colorado for college because I couldn't bear to be far from him, and I majored in biochemistry because I wanted to figure out what was happening with his brain chemistry. No one else could figure it out, so I decided I would. When he moved to a group home in Denver, I moved to the mountains and then to California; I couldn't call or text him to catch up, so I prayed, hard, that he'd have someone like a sister to fill the role I wasn't playing. To this day, I cannot articulate the profound gratitude — and envy -I feel for the women who answered those prayers, care providers who loved my brother as much as I did, the same way I did, when I couldn't be there to show it to him. I was desperately thankful that he wasn't alone. I remain desperately sad, and jealous, that other people, proxies for me, knew him better and spent more time with him than I did, thanks in part to my choice to live my own life. I always knew we'd have more time together later, but dammit, I was wrong. I'm going to miss how slowly and deliberately Christian moved. He floated around, like a Tai Chi master. I'll miss how tan he was, always, and how his hair lightened in the summer sun. I loved the way he signed Andrew's name, and how he said "Kels" and "Ovivia". And oh, his laugh -he had the best laugh. I'll miss how he watched things unfold, content in not being the center of attention, but constantly aware of what was going on -and when he'd had enough, he'd politely and silently just leave, ghosting his own family. I'll miss him for our future selves -especially my daughters. Olivia is too young to remember her time with him. I can't imagine what it'll be like to have our second next month without Uncle Christian visiting in the hospital. More than anything I'll miss how he was a full sixth of us. That's why it's so hard to say goodbye; we're not whole anymore. We never will be.

I can't think of how to close this; it feels unfinished. Like his life. I figured someday I would say goodbye to Christian, but I never expected it would be this soon. I hate that I have 60 or more Christmases in front of me before I get to celebrate with him again. I'm sad for the world at what it's missing now that he's gone. I have peace in knowing that we both knew how much we loved each other, but I'll miss him every minute for the rest of my life.

Kelsey Sprowell published with permission

Ava's Inclusion Highs and Lows

Sally Fernandes

"We had to fight for inclusion all along the way, but it was well worth it, and I don't regret any of it." This is a quote I often hear from parents who have children with Down syndrome older than my daughter. We all look to those families who come before us for advice on this journey we're all taking. I can say for my daughter Ava, soon to be nine years old, that in 2018 we're still fighting for aspects of inclusion, but yes, it is well worth it.

I thought the best way to convey our journey would be to point out some high and low points, but you will see in the end the highs tip the scale:

HIGH: Inclusion for Ava started at age four, when our school district's preschool director asked if we'd like to place Ava in the class with typical students, not the special services class. I was overjoyed that I didn't even have to ask for this placement; inclusion seemed almost too good to be true. The year progressed, and kindergarten registration was approaching. In my mind, I was conjuring how to ask for inclusion for Ava at our neighborhood school where my two older kids also attended. To my pleasant surprise, the same preschool director approached me again with the thought of placing Ava in kindergarten at our neighborhood school. Again, I didn't even have to ask! Kindergarten was a wonderful experience with an amazing teacher who never hesitated to have a student with special needs, treating Ava just like everyone else. Ava made bonds with several friends and rooted the beginning of her "celebrity status" on campus with her outgoing and social nature.

HIGH: The district's administrators have always been good about granting my requests for Ava's teachers. Some of her teachers have been my older kids' former teachers and some have been teachers I didn't know so well, but I did know they were not afraid to smile at Ava and say hi to her in passing on campus. Sometimes that's all I needed to know—that these teachers had the heart to spend a year with her. The TEACHERS every year have been the biggest asset to Ava's success.

LOW: First grade we were blessed with another great teacher, but we definitely had issues with Ava's behavior and getting the appropriate supports for her. This class had a half day aide due to language learners in the class, but no special services aide wasassigned. Over time, the aide was spending a lot of time attending to Ava's needs, and the teacher realized this is not what hertrue service was supposed to be. We agreed that Ava required an additional aide. That January was Ava's IEP where I requested an aide, but the district was hesitant to provide someone for her. At that same IEP, the school psychologist suggested Ava attend the special day class, which was on a different campus. This statement is one of those that makes your heart drop, and my husband and I were not so quick to give in to moving Ava. We tried to remain open-minded and asked if we could go observe this class. When we toured, it took very little time for my husband and I to realize this was NOT the place for Ava. The teacher was very nice and the instruction towards IEP goals was very organized, but the class structure was much like a preschool, and that would be going backwards for Ava. It seemed somewhere along the ranks the district was not addressing LRE and FAPE for Ava, not using their resources to help Ava succeed in her current placement. My husband and I made it clear that we would not agree to move Ava.

LOW: The school psychologist tried to use outdated jargon, such as "an aide for Ava would single her out and make her feel different," and "she will learn her goals much faster in the special day class." Our response to that was that all the students already know that Ava is different and has special needs, so she's already singled out, but it's not a big deal! They love her, love to play with her, and love to help her. Also, she's going to probably learn the same IEP goals at either placement, but learn more from her typically-developing peers, and that makes all the difference.

HIGH: In this same timeframe, as Ava's behavior issues were escalating, the district was NOT quick to address her needs with a behavior specialist or interventions. Her RSP teacher, however, did put together a daily behavior chart to encourage Ava to make good choices, and I appreciated this because it became a good mode of communication and record keeping between home and school. This behavior chart became standard use for other students with special needs as well, and a version of that chart is still used for Ava today.

HIGH: Not until the spring of first grade did a special services aide finally get assigned to Ava. She was amazing!!! This aide was very experienced and knew all the tricks to get Ava to work and make good choices. Better late than never, but things were headed in the right direction.

LOW:: Second grade, another amazing teacher, and even though the district agreed to place a special services aide in the class, they gave Ava a terrible match. This lady was more like a sweet grandma, and openly admitted that she had a hard time saying "no" to Ava. That's like giving Ava a free pass to bad behavior!

HIGH: Luckily the teacher took the reins with the district in quickly getting this aide switched, as she knew this first aide was not effective at all and it affected the dynamics of her whole class. A second aide came in and although she was young and inexperienced, Ava liked her. There was a definite learning curve the rest of the year, though, because Ava would try to take advantage of this young sweet aide. Our children with Down syndrome figure out very quickly how to bend the rules! Although there were bumps along the road, Ava had an overall good year, learning a lot and strengthening her social skills.

HIGH: Third grade got off to a great start with a wonderful teacher and another new aide. This aide happened to be a family friend that Ava was already familiar with, so this was like a dream team! The teacher and aide knew exactly how to talk on Ava's level and were not afraid to be firm with her when necessary. Ava was not going to win any battle of the wits with these two!

LOW: Unfortunately, the district does not hire full-time aides, so a different aide fills in in the morning. Ava, of course, found a way to take advantage of this young, inexperienced aide. Over the course of a few months the teacher and I were discussing how to address the issue. We wondered if these aides were given any kind of training to work with special needs students. Come to find out, the answer was NO! Even as a veteran teacher, she had to attend a training for special needs the summer before school started, but the aides had no support.

HIGH: The district's behavior specialist was now planning to meet with the aides and spend some time shadowing them to guide appropriate actions with the students. Sometimes it takes a low to make a high—it's always going to be a learning curve!

In our journey, we have definitely learned that staying involved and being your child's advocate is a necessity. Every child has different needs, so inclusion is going to look different for everyone. Ava is pulled out of her regular class twice a day for thirty minutes each time to work with the RSP teacher on math and reading. Some may push for all instruction to be fully included within the classroom, but I agree with this specialized time for her. She's getting the benefits of both worlds.

What warms my heart most is watching her on campus with all the other kids, and they LOVE HER. I've even had parents and grandparents approach me to express how happy they are that their child is in class with Ava. This is what inclusion is all about!

Outside of school, Ava also participates in a number of "inclusion" activities. She's on her fourth year of dance at a dance studio with typical children. She has done ballet, tap, hip hop, and jazz. The studio owner has placed a teenage helper in the class at times for support, but this year Ava is in there with just her instructor and fellow dancers and it's going pretty well! The recitals are a highlight every year, and I get comments all around town for weeks afterward about how adorable Ava is on stage. In our church, Ava has taken catechism classes with typical children for four years now. I do personally stay as an aide for her. You have to be realistic in your expectations. When catechism is right after school and kids are tired, I can't expect to just drop Ava off and think she'd actually stay focused and well-behaved. She received her First Communion last year and now does a great job receiving Communion in church every Sunday. The priests and Eucharistic Ministers love watching her receive; it truly warms the heart.

Ava is so much a part of our community due much in part to being included in the same things the typical kids have access to. She's a local celebrity and has such a positive impact on everyone she meets. Although it can be daunting at times to advocate for inclusion, especially when we don't even have to think about these things for our typical children, it is well-worth it in the end. Our journey continues, more highs and lows to come for sure, but in the end Ava and the rest of us will be better off because of it!

Sally Fernandes is a wife and mother of three, the youngest with Down syndrome. They live in central California, and actively support anything related to the local DS community.

"it shouldn't matter how slowly a child learns as long as we are encouraging them not to stop."

~ Robert John Meehan

Parker Bradshaw: Inclusion Matters!

Kay Bradshaw

You know how they say a picture is worth a million words? If you have an extra nine minutes, search YouTube for Parker Bradshaw: Inclusion Matters. This is what it's all about!

It has been our experience through the years that the absolute best place for Parker to be is with his peers in a typical classroom a high percentage of the day. This is the world our kids grow up in. Why should it be different if you have Down syndrome? What better way to get them accustomed to friendship, good behavior, respect, challenges, and success?!! Our experience has been that the nicest and smartest kids in the class are usually the ones who clamored to be Parker's helper in the classroom, lunchroom, and playground. Now that Parker has grown up to the ripe old age of twenty (how did that happen?) we stand by that decision!

At the beginning of Parker's junior year in high school, he came to me and asked if he could run for student council (STUCO).

He already had a very full schedule with no room for another class, so I talked him into waiting until his senior year and then we would 'talk about it.' I figured he'd forget about it the next year. Hahaha! The first week of his senior year, he came home with a packet to run for STUCO. It was already filled out by him. He had already received all his teachers' signatures. What else could we do but sign it and let him turn it in?

It was a full-blown campaign: posters, sticker handouts, and a speech on the school T.V. Parker chose the office he wanted to run for—Public Relations. He knew that if he won, he would get to lead the pledge twice a week on the microphone for the whole school to hear. (Thank you, dear speech therapists!!!!) He won hands-down! Now let me tell you that he ran unopposed, but it did not matter to him! I kind of think no one else dared run against him. He had the best year of his life as a senior being a part of the leadership, being a member of the swim team, being in the school orchestra, going to the dances, and ultimately being crowned prom king at the end of the year. Inclusion matters!!

Kay Bradshaw is a mother of nine children. Parker, who has Down syndrome, is the youngest and has been a delightful part of the family and the community

More Alike Than Different

Melanie Farmer

Last month Grady asked if he could take Gretchen in for show-and-tell. It was sooo sweet!

I told him we should wait until October and he could even read a book to his classmates. He was super excited, so I reached out to his homeroom teacher Mrs. Brown. She had to check the rules on such a presentation. It was approved!

Grady started reading 47 Strings, everyday practicing it (he even changed Cassin and Tessa's names to Grady and Gretchen!) We decided to mix blue and yellow Sixlet candies with M&M's and to talk about how we are all different on the outside, but made up of basically the same things on the inside. Mrs. Brown asked if both his homeroom class and his secondary classmates could be included, and of course the more the merrier. She did a little research herself and learned about how we all wear crazy socks on 3.21, and got paper socks for the kids to color in wacky ways to hang on the wall outside their classroom for the whole month of October!

There were so many questions from the kids, (50 of them) but what stuck out the most to me, is none of them would have even thought anything was different about Gretchen without us telling them.

Grady read his story and did such a great job. He is and will always be her best friend, biggest cheerleader, motivator, guide and big brother. #dssiblings #theluckyfew #advocateandinspire #gretchenannefarmer

Melanie Farmer is a work from home mom to two kiddos, Grady is almost ten, and Gretch who has DS is three. They live in rural Arkansas and love country livng.

Willow: Inspiring the Next Generation

Jennifer Hines

"Bye, Willow!"

It's something I've heard probably a thousand times. But this time, it was different. This time the words were felt, not just heard.

They came from a little boy on Willow's first day of preschool. That was a hard day for me. From my perspective, I had just put my small, fragile, beautiful three-year-old daughter in the middle of a scary, unfamiliar place, full of judgmental children. It took everything in me to walk out of that classroom without her. Honestly, the only reason I did was because Willow wanted to stay.

In fact, she was so excited she didn't even say goodbye.

I spent the next three hours crying, worrying that she was being picked on. Her classmates might not know she has Down syndrome, but surely they can see Willow's differences. She's half their size, after all. She doesn't talk either. Then there's her walking. Ugh. She's three, in a classroom of three- and four-year-olds and she doesn't walk. She doesn't even crawl. She scoots. On her bottom. Surely, they'd laugh at that. How could she not stand out?

She did.

It became very clear, the minute I arrived to pick Willow up. She most definitely did stand out. But it wasn't because of her differences.

"Oh, she is such a sweetheart!"

"I just want to stick her in my pocket and take her home with me!"

Those were the comments from her teachers. I guess I expected that. But, what about her peers? What did they think? Did I dare ask?

"She just had so much fun, today! She's right where she belongs." One of her teachers said. I still didn't understand, as I scooped up Willow to take her home. And then I heard it, as I walked out the door.

"Bye, Willow!"

It came from the locker area. It was a little boy, one of Willow's classmates. Or I guess I should say, her friend.

That little boy's enthusiastic goodbye passed straight through my ears down into my heart. And then I looked at Willow's face.

She was smiling. She had a good time at school. More importantly, she had made a friend. Or, I guess I should say, friends.

Willow was so excited as we pulled into the school parking lot that following week. She was grinning ear to ear.

"Willow!" I heard from the minivan next to us. It was a different boy this time. Another friend.

"Willow needs that to help her walk" I heard the little boy tell his mom. He was pointing to the fancy gold walker I was pulling out of the back of our van.

His words were just so matter of fact. They carried no emotion, no judgement. They were just a three-year-old's observations.

As we walked inside, Willow was greeted by more hellos. Her classmates were truly excited to see her. And Willow was equally excited to see them.

Seeing all her friends standing next to their lockers, Willow quickly looked for her walker. She climbed into it and walked right up to the classroom door, eager to get started on the day.

The minute the door opened, she was off. Her friends right beside her. And then it hit me. This is inclusion.

All my fears, all my emotions about sending Willow off into this world stem from my own childhood, where inclusion didn't really exist. I don't have any memories of children with special needs in my classes growing up, because most were put in separate classrooms. I may not have seen them, but I certainly heard about them, mostly in the form of jokes. Sadly, the R-word was real popular in my day. Things are different now. Thank God, things are different now!

Willow's differences don't separate her from her classmates. They also aren't the main reason she stands out. No, that's her personality. She's spunky and lovable!

Sure, her classmates notice her differences, but they aren't afraid of them, because they've been given the chance to know Willow, to play with her, and to become her friend. She's their classmate, their friend, all thanks to inclusion.

That goodbye I heard on the first day of school? It would have never happened without inclusion. That goodbye is proof that the new generation, Willow's generation, is different. Better. Beautiful.

That goodbye gave me hope. It warmed my heart. And it showed me what this world is becoming, that acceptance is growing and that love is winning.

Jennifer Hines is a wife and mother of three. She also runs a blog detailing the joys and challenges of raising a child with Down syndrome.

Anika: Teaching Self Reliance

Tabatha Tovar

When I think of inclusion, I think of joining my daughter to the greater community. My daughter was mainstreamed throughout elementary school and joined many afterschool programs including Girl Scouts. I believe that these experiences have increased her circle of friends, instilled compassion and respect for disabilities amongst her more typical friends, and increased her resiliency and ability to behave appropriately in the community. Here are three stories I would like to share:

1) When Anika was in fourth grade, I was leading her little sister's Girl Scout Troop. One day I was the only adult around and needed to lead these twelve first grade girls from school across the field to the recreation center for our Girl Scout meeting. I was very nervous about getting them all to the recreation center, as girls this age were like butterflies that fluttered in unpredictable ways. We arrived at the recreation center when I realized that Anika hadn't followed us and was left at school! Leaving the Girl Scouts with the other adults I rushed back to the school in a panic. She was probably alone and probably scared and lost or worse – maybe she walked out on her own and was now wandering the streets looking for me and putting herself in danger! When I got to the school I found her sitting on the ground with two of her classmates playing a game. She was perfectly happy and perfectly safe. The girls said that Anika was sitting by herself so they went to hang out with her for a little while until their parents came. My heart was so happy!

2) One of the nice things about having my daughter be a part of typical groups is her lack of special treatment. That sounds unkind, but hear me out. My daughter is in "special" education programs

and "special" Olympics and often gets "special" treatment from adults who are giving her special privileges due to her Down syndrome (much to her siblings' annoyance). My long-term vision of her does not include just getting an extra piece of candy at the grocery story but having an interesting, productive life, and that sometimes means waiting in lines or forgoing what is easy, for something more satisfying in the long run. I don't want her to be treated "special" for brief periods of time by various groups, rather I want her to be involved in those groups. When Anika was in Girl Scouts, she became just another member of the group. All of the girls had various strengths as well as areas of challenges. When they went camping, her troop leader had high expectations of everyone pitching in and working to the best of their ability. Anika was no exception.

One night everyone was lining up for dinner and my daughter wanted to cut ahead of the line and be first. At school she often gets to be first whenever she wants, but if she's going to work some day at a regular job, she needs to sometimes be second or third or even last. The girls in her group like her and are very friendly with her but they also wanted to eat. When she ran to the front of the line they told her that she'd have to wait like everyone else. This at first didn't go well and she dropped to the ground and cried. Her troop leader very calmly told her that it was ok to be upset but laying in the dirt was not okay. If she wanted to lay down, she could do so in the tent. If she wanted to eat, she could get in line. Her troop leader was calm and firm and, while this crying behavior often worked at school, Anika realized that she was not going to get her way there. Anika quickly sat up, brushed off the dirt, rewashed her hands, and got in line. When she had her food, her friends scooted over to let her sit in the middle of the group. No one made a big deal of it, and she let it go and had fun. She doesn't try to get her way by tantrums on the ground anymore. Now, she stands in line and gets what she wants in ways that'll serve her well in the long run.

3) Resiliency and self-reliance are qualities I try to instill in all three of my children. In many ways, Anika will have more support throughout her life than my other two but, life doesn't always go as expected and she needs skills to figure out how to navigate unexpected situations. When Anika was in seventh grade, she spent half of the time in a special day class and half of the time in typical classes. We decided to have her meet me afterschool in front of the school instead of meeting in her special day class so that she could increase her independence. The first time we met that way, Anika walked out to the front grass, didn't see me and folded into a fetal position with her face into the grass. It took a while to find her but when I did we talked about her feelings and how to deal with them.

"Were you scared when you couldn't find me?" I asked, and she nodded. "Who is around that you can go to if you need help?"

We listed her teacher and her aide, as well as the office staff who could call me if she needed it. "Besides, you

don't have eyeballs in your butt so if you want to find me, you have to stand and look with your eyes." She laughed.

We eventually figured it out. She called from the office a couple of times but mostly she stood in front with the other students and found me with little trouble.

Flash forward a couple of years and Anika is now in high school. The first week of school we agreed on a meeting place. The first Wednesday, I misunderstood the schedule and thought it was a full day, but it was actually a half day. I was up the street from the school when I got a call from her cell phone.

"Mom, I'm waiting for you."

"Is everything ok?"

"School is over and it's time to go." Oh no! Half day!

I rushed to school and found her at the regular meeting place. There were a few other kids, so she wasn't totally alone. I asked her what she did when school was out and she couldn't find me.

"I talked to some friends but then they had to go. Then I talked to other friends but then they had to go. You weren't here so I texted you, but you didn't text back. Then I called you."

"If I hadn't answered the phone what would you have done?"

"Go to the office."

"Perfect, sweetie, perfect!"

I felt so proud of her. In this unexpected situation she didn't freak out or get scared. She found peers and occupied herself socially with those who knew her well from having her in class and activities throughout elementary and middle school. They welcomed her and she felt comfortable. When I still hadn't arrived, she reached out appropriately with her phone and had a back-up plan to get help if needed. What more can we want for our children— all of our children— to be cared for and accepted by their peers and have the resiliency to handle unexpected situations.

Tabatha Tovar is an aspiring author and mother of three through birth and adoption, the eldest of whom has DS. They happily live in California with three cats and an imaginary llama.

As a Principal

Susan Carter Rollins

I fondly remember growing up in a school in which inclusion took place. In our school, two grades were always combined and that allowed me to have Cedric in my classroom every other year. Cedric had special needs (and abilities) and all of us saw it as an honor to be able to be in the same class as him and especially be the student who got to help him with his academics for the day. We all got along so well, and Cedric enjoyed the school and friendship experience. He gave us kindness, laughter, and fun. Looking back now, I see that in addition to the benefits for Cedric, it opened the minds of all of us as his classmates to the abilities and gifts of everyone.

As the principal of Highland Arts Elementary, a public school in Mesa, Arizona, we place an emphasis on using the arts to enhance student learning. We utilize music, drama, and visual arts along with dance to assist students in their learning of math, reading, and all subject areas. With our seemingly unique perspective on learning, it just seemed natural that we would fully include a student with Down syndrome into our regular classrooms and curriculum. From kindergarten until his parents (unfortunately) moved out of the city, Raymond was simply another member of our school community. Yes, there was some extra work to ensure that we placed him with the "right" teacher at each grade level, modified the standard curriculum, and selected an appropriate aide to help in his classroom, but all of it was simply a way to show our entire school community the value that every student brings.

It was always a great joy for me to see all of our classes sing and learn new songs, and Raymond, like most children, showed a love for music and was always active in music. We would hold student plays during the year with all involved students practicing after school. In fifth grade Raymond chose to try out for (and was selected to be in) the musical play Peter Pan. Students in his grade level at

Highland already knew and loved him and they rallied around him as he learned his lines and fully participated in the play and the six weeks of practice leading up to it. It was such a joy to see how hard all the children worked to get the dance steps, actions, and songs in sync with one another. They presented the play for the whole school and again for the public on two separate nights. Raymond was wonderful in his role and throughout the play in the chorus and dances. After that, he was recognized throughout the school by the students in other grades, and his friendship base became school wide.

He was also an excellent basketball player and always had a group on the court playing with him at recess. I enjoyed seeing his friendships and his excitement throughout all his years at Highland Arts Elementary. I would see the way students greeted Raymond at the beginning of the day and at the end, making special efforts to say goodbye. I loved the many friendships he had attained. The benefits of those friendships work both ways. Raymond's presence at our school was a blessing to us and to his fellow students as well.

Having worked at several districts during my thirty-six years in education, it is my experience that some district offices forget that students are individuals. The programs superintendents and administrators have developed for children with special needs are fine for some children, but others are more benefitted by inclusion. Some districts, because these special programs are in place, are not open to inclusion; these districts push the special education teachers and the principals to use those programs rather than inclusion. No one knows the special needs child better than the parents and, in my opinion, the individual child and his parents should drive the education of the child. Parents should not be afraid to advocate for what they feel is right for their child.

Susan Carter Rollins holds a master's degree plus 79 hours in Elementary Education, a Reading Endorsement, and Administrative certification. She served in education 36 years, 17 as a teacher (grade 5, grade 2, grade 1, kindergarten, media center), and 19 as a principal.

My Son Nate: Just Another Boy

Holly Simon

Nathaniel was born fifteen years ago. He is my fifth child.

At his birth, my husband immediately knew that he had Down syndrome.

My husband asked the nurse if she saw what he saw, and she agreed. At that point I had no idea what was going on. My husband came over to my bedside and told me that he thinks our son has Down syndrome. Unfortunately, the doctors and the nurses all began to hang their head, they lost eye contact with me, and then began to tell me that they were sorry. Once I held my son Nathaniel, I knew there was nothing to be sorry about. The books that I received from the hospital were so outdated. They were printed in the '60s. The books told me everything Nate wouldn't be able to do, and on day two I decided to throw the books away!

Nate received wonderful care, but I realized there was a gigantic gap with acceptance, inclusion, compassion, understanding, awareness, and love. I decided early on that no one would ever say sorry to my son again. I began a foundation to educate anyone who would listen that our children are more alike than they are different. I literally began on my kitchen table with a dream. Ten years later our mission is now nationwide. All of our children deserve a congratulations at birth. They deserve the same opportunities as every child. I would love to say the road has been easy, it has not. My son Nate, also known as Nate the Great, is very well spoken, articulate, and has a great personality! He is known as the mayor of Chicago, as he is just a bundle of friendliness.

But unfortunately, the phone doesn't ring for play dates. Nate is now fifteen years old and even though we have made an impact on the world, sometimes things don't change. I know his peers love him, but they just don't include him. Nate has been included in everything, as we are large family. Nate is one of seven; we expect the same from him as everyone else. Nate gets no slack.

I fight every day for Nathaniel and for the millions of Nathaniels in the world. We need to understand that our children are merely children. They have feelings, likes, and desires, just like everyone else. I wish the world would become kinder and more understanding. I hope that by changing one person at a time we will get there.

Everything the books and the doctors told me Nate would not do, he has overcome. He has exceeded everything everyone has ever said. I am his loudest and best cheerleader, so that love and passion is felt by his teachers as well. Nate has been included in school. His teachers have always wanted the best for Nate, and at every IEP meeting we raise the bar higher and higher.

Nate is magical, no doubt about it. I just want the world to know how important our children are to our world.

Nate plays all sports and has over one hundred gold medals from Special Olympics. We've never allowed Nate to think he was any different than anyone else. Nate is just a boy.

We still have a long road for inclusion. Running a foundation that spreads the joy that our kids can bring often reminds me that many parents feel very defeated, as this is a very challenging road. I swear to these new moms: the road will be amazing. It will be hard but raising children, any child, is hard.

My goal started with wanting doctors and nurses to never say sorry again, now my goal is to bring opportunities to all those individuals that need more once school ends. In order to help with this vision, we began a bath and body products company that is run all by teens and adults with special abilities. It takes one person to do one thing to make a difference in this world; the ripple effect is incredible.

Holly Simon is a mom of five; her youngest has Down syndrome. Holly is a fierce advocate for all. A breast cancer survivor, she shoots from the hip. She is honest, raw, glittery, and kind.

Assuming Competence for Kayla

Michelle Helferich

We are a few months into the second school year of Kayla being at a private school, and I admit to sometimes still feeling bitter about how the whole transition-to-middle-school IEP meeting went with our local school district. The district's proposed placement was for Kayla to spend the vast majority of her school day in a self-contained classroom. This was a more restrictive placement than she had in elementary school.

I am so thankful that we had the opportunity, and the option, to send her to a private school where she is included for the vast majority of her school day. She doesn't go to math or ELA with her class, instead she goes to what is comparable to a Resource Room in the public schools.

The public middle school didn't even want to entertain the idea of Kayla being in a general education social studies and science class even though that was her placement during elementary school. And now not only is she in social studies and science, she is also in literature, religion, and Spanish classes.

She's included in a **foreign language class**! That wouldn't have even been an option for her in the public school (even though it is offered). The only classes she would have been included in were PE and band.

Does the fact that she's included in all those general education classes mean she is proficient in those subjects, keeping up with her class, and doing the exact same work as her classmates? Absolutely not, and she didn't have to be for her to be in the public school, either.

She does do the work that she is capable of—she participates in class and she takes tests that are modified to her level— but still on the exact same subject as the rest of the class. She takes a test on the same vocab words in literature that the class learned all week; she takes a test on key terms, people, and places in social studies. Her tests are matching or have a word bank, but they're still on the same material.

Do you know what being included means? It means she is challenged and **exposed to a wide variety and rich curriculum in general education.**

At the middle school IEP meeting, the special education teacher pointed out that Kayla would be the lowest level reader in her class … that she didn't have anyone in her class who was on a reading level "that low."

Nothing magical has changed Kayla's reading level since that meeting. She is still on an early-elementary reading level and she struggles with fluency, yet she still participates in literature class.

Last year her class read the novels *Holes; Chasing Vermeer; The Lion, The Witch and The Wardrobe*; and *Things Not Seen*. They didn't have to read these on their own; they were read together in class. The teacher would read the chapters and they would have a discussion. It wasn't until they were reading *The Lion* that Kayla mentioned taking a turn reading it. I asked her teacher what Kayla was talking about. He said the students took turns reading aloud from the book, they aren't required to read if they don't want to, and they can read as much or as little as they want. He said there were times Kayla did read out loud from the book. I pondered how that must have went— the copy we have is fairly tiny print and tracking words like that are hard for her. She doesn't know all of the words in the book but when she was having trouble pronouncing a word the student next to her would help her out. I lamented how that must have gone for the rest of the students; by the time they finished listening to Kayla read they probably had no idea what she just read (because, fluency). Her teacher reminded me that each student has their own copy of the book and are supposed to all be following along so they know exactly what is being read.

Not only did/does she participate in the discussion of the books, she took tests on them as well. Were her questions as involved and detailed as her classmates' test? No, but it was still on the subject of the novels and she was still able to answer specific questions.

We also read the books to her at home and, when available, listened to the audio book. Last year she recognized the cover of *Chasing Vermeer* in the audio books section of the library, so we checked it out and listened to it on our trip to Maryland. This year we've read, and listened to, *Maniac MaGee*, so when they start reading it in class she'll be familiar with it.

So just because she can't read any of those books on her own doesn't mean she shouldn't be exposed to them or that she can't be interested in them. Because she was familiar with *Things Not Seen*, when I saw *Things That Are* (with the same characters) at the library book sale, she wanted to get the book, and Joe is now reading it to her.

It's all about exposure and opportunities. She would have missed out on so much of this curriculum had she been in the self-contained classroom all day long.

This year they've read several short stories and teleplays out of their literature book, and Kayla has participated, too. She's been assigned a character in "The Monsters Are Due on Maple Street" (Rod Serling) and *The Hound of the Baskervilles* (Sir Arthur Conan Doyle) and she follows along and reads her part.

Because of being included, she's been Eris, Goddess of Chaos, in the sixth grade's Greek Museum presentation.

She's made projects like the Great Pyramids of Giza and a coat of arms. Can she do those projects on her own? No, I've had to help her with them ... but then she goes to class and presents her projects and talks about them just like everyone else.

Report cards just came out and she has all A's and B's. Her lowest grade is an 84 and her highest (not counting fine arts) is a 97. Again, this is not to misconstrue and insinuate that she is doing the amount of work her classmates are doing, but she is being graded on the work and tests she is given.

Yet she was deemed incapable of being in a general education classroom.

What about presuming competence and seeing what she could accomplish?

What about giving her a chance?

Instead of being immersed in, and exposed to, the same general education curriculum as her peers, our local district would have had Kayla learning to do laundry.

Michelle Helferich is a mom to two children, the oldest of whom has DS. They are a retired military family currently living in South Carolina.

Ripples

Erica Conway

When I think of my family's inclusion story, I'm not sure where to begin. I think it began on October 25, 2002, when I was seventeen weeks pregnant. The genetic counselor told me that my child, who we didn't even know the sex of, was going to have Down syndrome. When we were told to terminate this perfectly beautiful little life, that's when inclusion really began. Today Gretchen is fourteen and has been ever present in every aspect of our lives. She has been fully included since kindergarten at our local Catholic school with her two sisters. She has competed on swim teams, dance classes, basketball, track, and volleyball. All alongside her typical peers. She goes to school dances, and dances more than anyone else. She plans on getting her driver's license and to attend college just like her sisters.

I believe inclusion starts at home with an attitude. An attitude of the same goals and expectations for all of our children. They will be independent, happy adults, and our job is to give them the skills to do so and that starts with being involved in our community.

When we approached our Catholic school about Gretchen attending the principal looked at me and told me no one has ever asked her that before.

My advice for getting your child included is just ask. The answer just might surprise you. I am so proud to say that Gretchen is fully included in every aspect of life: the basketball team, group chats, and altar serving at church. Full inclusion also means high behavioral expectations. And, yes, Gretchen has lost her recess and, yes, Gretchen has been suspended because she knew what she was doing when she misbehaved, but she thought she could get away with it. Inclusion. The good and the bad. What I love about inclusion is the ripple effect.

When the bar is set high, they will reach the bar and then they will be included in more, and the expectations will rise, and all are forever changed. And more inclusion will follow. Be the pebble. For the ripples may become a tsunami.

Erica Conway is mom to three daughters: 18, 15, and 12. Gretchen (15) happens to have DS. They live in Napa, CA, where Erica practices dentistry.

A Brother's Perspective

Andrea Temarantz

We went to GiGi's Playhouse today to bring my youngest son, Ryder, to play group. Joe, my oldest son, was also with us.

I do talk to Joe about Down syndrome, but he definitely doesn't get it, so I don't push it.

After GiGi's, we went to the store, and on the way home Joe said, "Mom, does everyone that knows Ryder know he has Down syndrome?" I was shocked since he has never asked anything about it. I told him everyone that meets Ryder knows he has Down syndrome because it is easily noticeable.

He said, "It is? I think he's the cutest baby I've ever seen."

So I told him all the babies he saw today at GiGi's had Down syndrome.

He said, "They did? They are all so cute. Mom, my favorite is Gracie. How adorable is she?!? And that pink hat. It was so cute. She was rockin' it like a gangster!"

Andrea Temarantz is a mom to two boys who are best friends. Her youngest has DS. They live in Arizona and enjoy lots of fun in the sun.

Friends from the neighborhood for Nate

Jennifer Brownell

My son has been included in our neighborhood school since kindergarten. The gap is HUGE because he also has an autism diagnosis. We got this adaptive tricycle for him and I just HAD to share what happened for him the FIRST time we took a ride on it!! His friends from the neighborhood got up from what they were doing to greet him and cheer him on.

This would never happen if he was in a self-contained classroom in a different school in a different part of town.

Grateful for inclusion—worth the fight to have a moment like this!!

Jennifer Brownell is a warrior mama of two amazing boys; the oldest has a duel diagnosis of DS and autism. They live in Wisconsin and cherish both their DS and autism family.

Raymond and Baseball

Michelle and Stacy Tetschner

Our son Raymond currently attends Our Lady of Perpetual Help Catholic School in Scottsdale, AZ. This is our first year. He's in sixth grade.

When baseball season was getting started, we were excited for our son to join the team. Then we realized how complicated it could be. He does throw well, but isn't a good catcher, and it's unlikely he would be able to get a hit.

We let all the "what ifs" start to pile up. We let worry and fear get in the way.

We spoke with the coach, an amazing mom with four kids, who said, "Please let him play. I will make it work."

We were completely humbled by her faith in our son and her confidence that she could and would make it work. It was awesome! Our son was ecstatic to be a part of the team!

There were bumps along the way sure, but way too many wonderful highlights that we would have missed! One of the brightest moments for us, as parents, came when my son got up to bat at St. Thomas the Apostle School. He got a good solid hit, right to a player who then slowly and purposefully dropped the ball, allowing my son to get on base! This action wasn't "suggested," this wasn't "planned". This action was simple kindness and wonderful sportsmanship, in that one incredible moment! There are so many heroes in the world, from our coach to that player.

Inclusion isn't that complicated. It's simply choosing to concentrate on each other's gifts and strengths.

It's celebrating how perfect and unique we were all created.

Michelle and Stacy Tetschner 2016

She's Too Little!

Maria Jordan MacKeigan

At twenty weeks pregnant, we found out that our baby would be born with Down syndrome. I was devastated and fell into this big black hole of despair.

By the time Jordan Grace was born we were so in love with her, we forgot all about her disability. We were focused on getting to know our sweet little lady.

When she turned two years old, I fully jumped in with two feet into the Down syndrome community. I wrote and published my first children's book, A Princess Wish, based on my daughters. I also joined our local Down syndrome society.

The next summer I stumbled upon a post on Facebook about a school that was open for new student registrations. It was for 3- to 4-year-olds who would benefit from speech and occupational therapy.

I reached out to the person in charge, even though I was not ready to let my daughter fly. I thought she was way too young and too little in size. The lady was so encouraging. I told her I wasn't ready, and that I didn't think Jordan Grace was ready. She told me it would be great for her; I kept resisting. I told her I would need to volunteer and be there with her; she said it was open-door policy and that I could be in the classroom the entire time if I wanted.

Finally, we were ready. A month later, Jordan Grace was on her way to her first day of school. The teachers were beyond excited to have her in the classroom. She was the only one with Down syndrome.

Most of the staff had never known anyone rocking an extra chromosome, which was wonderful—not only was my baby girl learning from others, but others were learning from her!

Fast forward to the present. It is her second year at this preschool and she's more loved, included, and supported than ever.

The teachers miss her when she's gone, they celebrate each milestone as if she was their own, and the kids love and accept her for who she is.

It is such a blessing to be in a place where Jordan Grace can grow and succeed at her own pace.

Maria Jordan MacKeigan is a mother of two precious girls and married to a supportive husband. Author of a children's book, A Princess Wish. *A devout Down syndrome advocate.*

Dancing to Inclusion

Leticia Avena

Hi. My name is Leticia and my husband's name is Jesse. We are the proud parents of two amazing young adults with Down syndrome. Jessica is twenty-three years old. Isaiah is twenty-one years old and he has a dual diagnosis of Down syndrome and autism. Because they grew up and went to school with their typical peers, we knew there would be situations where they would have to be trailblazers. We knew that at times things might be tough, but we have never let them use their diagnosis as an excuse not to try something new or difficult. Their entire lives we have taught them that they can do whatever they set their mind to, but it just might take them a bit longer. We have always done everything in our power to help them reach their goals. So why on this one December night when Isaiah had a simple request was I so scared to help him try to fulfill it?

It was December of 2013, when we went to an old-town Christmas festival. There were various activities and performances to entertain the entire family. Because of the long lines at most of the booths, we decided to sit and watch the various groups perform on stage. Surprisingly, it was a group of Mexican ballet Folklorico dancers called Lindo y Querido that caught Isaiah's attention. He was mesmerized by the dance. He had never taken such an interest in anything like he did with this group. He said," Mom, I dance?" I said, "okay, Buddy." When the show was over, we left and I thought he would forget about it. When January came around I expected that he would have forgotten, but he continued to ask about dance. A couple of weeks went by before he finally stopped asking.

December of the following year, we went back to the same old-town Christmas festival. We were going to watch a play, but Isaiah had other plans. He led us over to the stage where we watched and waited. I had forgotten about the group, but Isaiah knew what he was waiting for. Luckily for Isaiah, the group is a regular at the festival. When Lindo y Querido took the stage, there was a look of excitement Isaiah's face. Once again he watched in amazement as the dancers performed. When their performance ended we tried to leave, but this time Isaiah refused to go. He kept saying, "talk to the lady." We would reply "Let's go see the show first, then we will come back." He knew that if we left, the group would be gone and so would his chance to dance. So we waited. Only when we truly spoke to someone from the group and got the director's contact information would he agree to leave.

I figured that with the holidays, he would once again forget. But every day he would say, "mom call dance lady please." To that I would reply, "okay bud, next week." This went on for a few weeks. Finally, around February when I realized he wasn't going to give up, I made the call. I just asked when and where they practiced and didn't mention anything about Isaiah, Down syndrome, or autism. I worried that if I told them, they wouldn't give him a chance. At first I couldn't figure out why I was hesitating. Then after much soul searching, I realized that I was afraid that he would be rejected or that he would fail.

So it was in March when we could go to our first practice. I asked Jesse, my husband, to take him; I worried I wouldn't be able to handle seeing him fail. That one hour that he was gone seemed like an eternity. I didn't know what to expect when they got home. To my surprise, Isaiah was ecstatic, and Jesse had that 'proud dad' look on his face. My heart was happy when Jesse told me that Isaiah had done well and was asked to join the group.

After a few weeks of practice and seeing how excited Isaiah was, Jessica decided that she also wanted to dance. Again I felt the same fear, and questions raced through my mind. Would Jessica be able to learn the dances? Would she be able to keep up since she has bad knees? Would she fail and be devastated? Again I was pleasantly surprised; she too was accepted into the group. It has been a bit more challenging for her, but everyone has been very patient with her.

Because of health issues, Jessica is still in the beginner group, but also practices with the intermediate group. She enjoys dancing, but it's not her main focus. For Isaiah, dancing ballet Folklorico is his passion. He proves it every time he dances, be it practice or a real performance.

While making the transition from the beginner to intermediate group, he was required to practice with both classes. That meant back-to-back practices—two hours of non-stop dancing. By the end of class, his clothes would be drenched in sweat, yet he was happy. Not once did he give up or complain. The maestro (his dance instructor) and the group director both took notice of his passion and hard work. This past December, he was rewarded by being crowned Lindo y Querido's king. Isaiah had always dreamed of being crowned prom king, which actually almost happened. (He lost by a few votes, but that's another story.) But this was even better. This wasn't based on popularity, but on his efforts. That day I realized that my fear of rejection could have kept my kids from achieving their dreams. My fear of seeing them fail could have kept others from seeing them succeed.

This March will be four years since they joined the group. It has been an awesome experience to watch them perform alongside their typical peers. When they take the stage, initially people are curious, but by the time they're done dancing, people are impressed. They no longer see two dancers with Down syndrome, they just see two dancers who are part of an amazing and accepting dance group.

Leticia Avena is a mom to two young adults with DS. They live in Peoria, AZ, where they are very active in their community.

What Would You Tell Teachers?
Why is Inclusion Important?

Lisa Windette Carey - Because we don't live in a segregated world.

Lisa L. Prusak - Inclusion benefits all students, not just students with disabilities. Everyone benefits from learning from one another. Differentiated education allows the children who learn faster to teach the ones who need more time. Everyone wins as the student becomes the teacher and also learns from his/her peers with disabilities what they can do and not what they can't do.

Susan Hadeishi - Inclusion is important because it teaches values, compassion, and things a computer can't teach. Inclusion teaches valuable lessons for all students, which will make them better humans, and it requires you to teach better as you rethink your message. It prepares the special child for the real world. Inclusion rocks for everyone when done right!

Melissa Bryant Watson - Kids brought up with a child with a disability don't see the disability. They see a kid. They are better helpers, kinder to each other, and more willing to include new friends.

Brooke Varma - I would want teachers to know that, most of the time, if inclusion is seen as a failure, it's due to poor planning and inadequate supports/accommodations. It also has to be meaningful to matter, so inclusion for the sake of checking a box to say you've done it is not genuine inclusion and doesn't benefit anyone.

Karen Ford Cull - I have talked to many experts on education and every single one of them has told me that in 30-40 years of research there is zero evidence that a segregated classroom offers any educational benefit. There are studies on the damage that segregated environments do to children with Down syndrome that show a signifi-cant impact compared to inclusive environments. There are also studies that show that one of the biggest indicators of future em-ployment for people with intellectual disabilities is the extent to which they were included in general education as a child. According to ARC, 85% of adults with intellectual disabilities are unemployed. There are over 270 college programs in the US that allow a individ-uals with ID to attend college and often participate in regular class-es. If college professors can do it, as well as Catholic schools, and charter schools - can't you?

Stephanie Mefford - Parents are partners. Without communication (daily or weekly), parents do not know what to reinforce, review, or reteach as needed. This lack of communication and partnership with the parents slows down the pace of the child's learning/education.

Julie Blaskovich - Assume competence AND spend that moment to decide the least amount of support that will set them on the path to independence followed by monitoring the path to independence that you identified. Try something, then contact me. We can either celebrate because what you tried worked or we can brain storm some other things for you to try. Sometimes you have exactly the right medicine, but the dose was too small, and they simply need more of your perfect solution dosed with extra consistency and patience.

Robbin Thomas Lyons - I would warn them that parents come with baggage. Before their child comes to you they have seen their child judged, told "no" many times, had to fight for services. They are worn down and worried that they will still have to fight for inclu-sion. They love their children. They wear boxing gloves sewn to their hands. They have to roll with the punches. Don't punch. Reach out to them and be a partner. Make them know that you want to help their child. You will fight for their child. You are on their side. De-fuse that bomb. Own that child as your student. Be their teacher.

Aides should not be the teacher. They are there to step in and help, but these kids look up to you. Make them know that you value them. And if they do not always act as they should, remember that those behaviors are not so much just a kid being bad, they are often a child begging for help and not knowing how to communicate their wants, needs, and desires.

To Parents Raising Inclusive Kids

Jessica Crain

To all the parents taking deliberate actions every day to shape caring, inclusive children, this "thank you" is for you.

To the parents raising children who refuse to let a classmate eat alone, I appreciate you.

To the parents whose daughter always watches out for her peers and makes sure everybody is included—thank you!

To the parents raising a son who asks everybody to join the game so nobody will have to stand on the sidelines alone—way to go!

For all the parents who raise kids who use kind and encouraging words with their peers and never put anybody down for their differences—I applaud you.

For the parents who don't shush their kids when they point out differences, but instead take the time to talk with their children and teach them that our differences should be celebrated because differences make the world interesting and beautiful—you are making a positive impact.

And for all parents who model inclusive, kind behavior because you understand your children are watching—job well done!

From a parent of a child with Down syndrome to all the parents raising children with kind hearts and open minds, I thank you from the bottom of my heart! Being the parent of a child with Down syndrome can be a vulnerable and lonely place, but it is from this place that I have developed a deep appreciation for exceptional parents. It takes the kindness of a whole community to ensure my son will have the opportunities he deserves in order to reach his personal best, and that can be nerve-racking.

Let's all keep working hardest at our most important job: parenting our children. It isn't easy, but with our attentive and kind parenting today, we are helping to change the world and give our kids (with and without disabilities) a brighter future. After all, we are all in this together!

Jessica Crain is a mom of two boys. Her eldest son is funny, smart, and also happens to have DS. Jessica is an advocate for individuals with DS and inclusive education.

Our Daughter Kaelyn

Brandi Couch

Our daughter Kaelyn is ten years old and has Down syndrome. It has been quite a learning experience since she entered the school system at the age of three. I remember sitting at her IEP meeting when she was about to transition from preschool to kindergarten. Of course, they were rushing through it, trying to finish within thirty minutes. At this point we really didn't know much, and didn't know our own or our daughter's rights. We did know we wanted as much inclusion as possible. At the end of the IEP, we told them we had expected and wanted more inclusion. Their only response was "well, she'll go to music and PE, that's inclusion."

We pushed back and got her into the gen ed classroom—a little more than just PE and music!

However, that first year of kindergarten she didn't make a lot of progress academically, so we chose to repeat kindergarten for another year. Within the first month of that next school year, it was brought to light that our daughter and other students in the self-contained classroom were being mistreated by the staff in that classroom. Through a series of events that led to us filing due process, we were fortunate enough to have a parent advocate and attorney who taught us how to advocate for our and our daughter's rights that we didn't even know we all have!

As a result, Kaelyn now spends at least 75% of her day in gen ed and the time she is in the self-contained classroom is quality time, mostly one-on-one time, working on those skills and goals she is very behind in.

She is also well known by just about everyone in her school and can list many friends (most of them from gen ed). Everyone tells us how much they enjoy her and how fun, funny, and caring she is. At her previous school where the abuse was occurring, we were starting to see behaviors from her, and I was getting worried. But once we found the reason for that and the abuse stopped, her behaviors stopped, too. When they put appropriate interventions in place for her after obtaining thorough and appropriate assessments, the behaviors went away and she started thriving.

At her new school you can tell she is a part of that community and not just shoved off in some separate classroom all day. This year she is making big strides in her reading and writing. She has also attended the after-school program for the last few years with success. She is the only one with special needs who attends the program at her school.

Kaelyn has also participated in a dance class at the local community college for the last 5 years. Kaelyn has also done ballet, tap, jazz, and hip-hop classes. Of course, hip-hop is her favorite!

When she started the class, she was not yet potty trained, which is a requirement for the class; however, they did not make it an issue and we were always on hand to assist. Her teacher worked it out with us that if she needed us, they would text me to come back and assist, but it was never needed. Kaelyn has thrived in this class and loves being on stage! She does the dance moves as well as, if not better than, some of the other girls! She loves her teacher, and her teacher holds her to the same standards as the other students. I remember when we went to the first Watch Day, Kaelyn was kind of showing off, not really listening to the teacher (mostly because I was there!). I told her teacher after class, "Don't let her get away with that! If she isn't doing what you expect, make her do it!" Her teacher looked a little surprised, but we have high expectations for Kaelyn! Down syndrome or not!

Kaelyn is also the member of a Girl Scout troop with typical girls. Kaelyn is a very social child and loves the social interaction her troop provides. Girl Scouts was recommended to us by her occupational therapist. I kind of drug my feet in signing her up, worried that we would have push back once they found out she has Down syndrome. I feared that they might have a "special needs troop" they would make her sign up for. Then I was contacted by a friend who was starting a troop for her daughter! Her daughter and Kaelyn had been in Kindermusik together when they were toddlers, and my friend had heard we were thinking about signing Kaelyn up. She welcomed Kaelyn with open arms to their troop and has been accommodating when needed. We have been to many council events and so impressed with how Kaelyn is treated. Kaelyn sells cookies during cookie season and works cookie booths. She may not be able to handle the money quite yet, but she can charm the pants off of anyone and convince them to buy cookies! And the other girls help her with the money part. They work well as a team.

We have high expectations for our daughter and expect others to have them, too. We feel if you have high expectations, a person will strive to meet them, pushing them to reach their potential. Inclusion at school and in the community helps her reach her potential as long as everyone continues to have high expectations for her! She is capable of so much!

Brandi Couch is mom to Kaelyn, age ten, who has DS, and wife to Aaron. They live in Texas and enjoy chauffeuring Kaelyn to her social events!

"I think the hardest part of having a child
with a delay of any kind is the fight:
The fight for services.
The fight for people to understand
who your child is and what they need.
The fight for knowledge,
because knowledge is power.
And the quiet fight you have within yourself
wondering if you've left no stone unturned."
~ Jessie Doyle

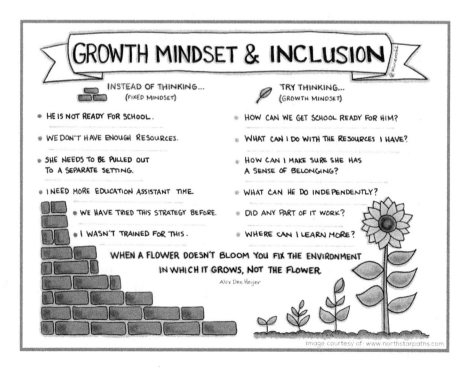

GROWTH MINDSET & INCLUSION

INSTEAD OF THINKING... (FIXED MINDSET)	TRY THINKING... (GROWTH MINDSET)
HE IS NOT READY FOR SCHOOL.	HOW CAN WE GET SCHOOL READY FOR HIM?
WE DON'T HAVE ENOUGH RESOURCES.	WHAT CAN I DO WITH THE RESOURCES I HAVE?
SHE NEEDS TO BE PULLED OUT TO A SEPARATE SETTING.	HOW CAN I MAKE SURE SHE HAS A SENSE OF BELONGING?
I NEED MORE EDUCATION ASSISTANT TIME.	WHAT CAN HE DO INDEPENDENTLY?
WE HAVE TRIED THIS STRATEGY BEFORE.	DID ANY PART OF IT WORK?
I WASN'T TRAINED FOR THIS.	WHERE CAN I LEARN MORE?

WHEN A FLOWER DOESN'T BLOOM YOU FIX THE ENVIRONMENT
IN WHICH IT GROWS, NOT THE FLOWER.
Alex Den Heijer

image courtesy of: www.northstarpaths.com

Retaining in Kindergarten
Pushing for Inclusion

Michelle Tetschner

Our vision for inclusion started when my son was just little. When our son was young, we searched out older children and youth with Down syndrome around the country. We looked for self-advocates that were good speakers, those who were truly advocating for themselves and the Down syndrome community. We asked questions, and the main commonality we found? They were fully included in school!

This became our goal!

We had to learn early on, to be strong in our commitment to that vision.

We had almost completed kindergarten and were at our spring IEP. The team suggested that we look at a co-taught program at another school. While we were not excited about moving our son, we were open to the idea. We trusted their recommendations and went to tour the new school. The teacher seemed amazing, and the idea of co-teaching was very intriguing. We agreed to try the program in the fall. When fall came, the teacher we had met in the spring seemed very different. She was not outgoing and happy but appeared overwhelmed and frustrated. I didn't know what to do or think. I was able to observe that first week and was very disappointed with what I was seeing. Nothing was glaringly obvious, but the staff and children seemed very unhappy, out of sorts, and no one seemed to know what was next or who was in charge of what. I tried to remain optimistic.

I went back the following week and was only planning to stay for a short time, but I stayed for 1.5 hours. I didn't want to leave my son there. When I asked questions about the "co-teaching" program that we had signed up for, I was told that this plan had changed. There were now too many kids in the special ed portion of the class and now they would only do a co-teaching program 2-3 times a week for social studies only, for only thirty minutes, and he would be in the self-contained room the rest of the time. This is not what we had signed up for. I left in tears, taking my son out early for the day, knowing I couldn't send him back there again.

I called for an IEP meeting the next day.

Keeping the story short, we had the IEP meeting. It went badly. In my memory, I can still clearly see the older male school psychologist stand up and angrily say, "How dare you question my expertise!" and "I know what is best for your child! I have been doing this for over 50 years." and "No, I have not met your son, but I have read his file."

I got up and left the meeting after that statement. Sobbing. I could barely drive home. I was so angry and so sad. I was so upset and so very disappointed in our school system. How could they honestly think they know my son better than me? And how could they possibly think they know what is best for my child? When they hadn't even met him?

After lengthy discussions with the school district, we were able to go back to our old school, back to the principal who adored my son, and we repeated kindergarten again. With the principal smoothing the way, we were able to get back on track. Our teacher that year was open to the idea of having my son in her class and she quickly fell in love with my son, the same as she did with all her other students.

By repeating kindergarten, my son was able to keep up many times during that second year.

Because he was repeating, he knew the routine and knew the expectations. He was more confident, was able to be a line leader and was able to navigate the school grounds. He was able to feel successful and grew more confident each day.

My son, like many kids with Down syndrome, loves routine. He loves to know what is next and what is coming later.

Repeating kindergarten allowed many of those fears and worries to be alleviated because he knew what was coming-he had done it before!

Academically, he did awesome.

He had already been through this once! Now these numbers and letters that he was learning were repeat material for him and in that second year his growth matched many of the lower students in his class.

He made slow and steady progress and he gained social skills like crazy! He was loved by all his peers. He was greeted enthusiastically every morning and was often found walking hand in hand with peers to and from the playground.

Children with Down syndrome learn by watching and practicing and are especially good at mimicking their peers. They learn social cues from seeing interactions and copying them. Having him be around his gen ed peers, hearing their rich language, and seeing them in action is vital to how my son learns best.

Looking back-we are so grateful to that school and principal. The foundation that was built in those years, has carried through to today.

There is simply no stopping my son when he wants to do something. He can be very driven and motivated if the subject interests him. He has been in several school plays, has played on school basketball and baseball teams, and is getting B's for grades. He is also a good reader and loves to do his accelerated reading books and tests. One of his favorite positive behavior rewards was reading with a peer of his choice! He adores science and doing the labs with his fellow students. He is great at memorizing his study/Dolce words, though he may only have 8-10 words compared to the 20-25 words that the other students have. His academic growth continues to be steady and strong, and we have been lucky to find educators who will meet him where he is and grow from there.

There is another side to this story—what about the gen ed students? It's amazing when you can step back and see what a wonderful teacher my son is for his fellow students. His peers have learned how to interact with him, how to help him, and how to be friends with him. They have learned compassion, patience, and kindness. These students are our future doctors, lawyers, nurses, and teachers, and they need to know how to be around all neuro diverse types of people. They will be the people to hire my son, work with my son (and others with special needs) and be his friend and neighbor.

For us, we looked to the future. For us, using a second year of kindergarten at the beginning of his education was logical. We looked at it as building a firm foundation. We know that my son wants to go to college just like his brothers. When that IEP meeting happened 10 years ago, a college program didn't seem like an option. But now there are over 260 college programs for people with disabilities, and that number is growing. My son states clearly that he wants to go to college, just like his brothers.

My son is now fourteen and is still fully included at his school in the seventh grade. It hasn't always been easy to convince each teacher and school just how amazing my son can be. People are often amazed at all that he can do and all that he can learn, once they open their hearts and minds to how he truly wonderful he is.

My son is more than a diagnosis, he is a boy who happens to have Down syndrome.

Pushing for inclusion has been a somewhat bumpy journey, but completely worth it.

We all live together in one world.

We all just want to belong, be successful, and be loved.

#MoreAlikeThanDifferent

Michelle Tetschner 2016

Our Son Trevor

Robert Hendershot

My dear son Trevor,

I recall the day of your birth, Friday, May 4, 1990, at first as one of the happiest, and then one of the saddest, and finally in retrospect one of the greatest days of my life, all in one. When I first saw you being born and the doctor said, "He's a boy!" that was the happiest moment of my life. But when that same doctor, five minutes later, asked me, "Do you know what Down syndrome is?" that was one of the saddest moments of my life. I was so angry with God, "I don't deserve a son like this!"

While I've apologized to you many times over the years, I'll always be so sorry for thinking and saying something like that. But you know that all the trials and triumphs, setbacks and successes we've experienced in our lives together over the last twenty-eight years have actually proved that I was right all along ... I really did not deserve a son like you Trevor, but for the completely opposite reason...

In elementary school, you were teased relentlessly until you finally had enough and yelled at your offender, "My daddy loves me! F*** you!" and flipped him off. The school was going to suspend you for screaming profanity and making an obscene gesture until I intervened and told them there would be severe consequences for you later. I hope you remember we both got three scoops of ice cream on the way home, and that was the end of that...

In middle school, we found out your para-educator was video-taping you singing Christian songs on the school bus. She wanted to humiliate you into stopping by showing everyone how "ridiculous" you looked and sounded, but you kept on singing anyway. Since then you've added clapping and dancing to your worship routine and you continue to inspire parishioners to tears at our church on Sunday mornings...

At the start of high school, you were bullied, called the 'r' word, and told you were worthless. And yet by your senior year you'd turned the whole school around to the point where the faculty drafted you onto the homecoming court, and then your classmates elected you homecoming king in the greatest landslide in school history—you received more votes than the other four candidates combined...

After graduating, you were told that the best job you could ever hope for would be folding towels in the basement of a hotel laundromat. Nevertheless, in 2012 you were hired by Major League Baseball's LA Angels and then in 2013 by the National Hockey League's Anaheim Ducks to be the greeter in their respective team stores. Over the years, you've become known, admired, and often loved by tens of thousands of sports fans, fellow employees, team executives, and professional athletes...

As you know, we recently formed a 501c3 non-profit corporation, Angels for Higher, *www.angelsforhigher.org* to facilitate the hiring of many more individuals with Down syndrome to work as greeters in many more sports venues across the United States, North America, and eventually around the world. Our vision is to transform the pro-life, special needs culture of the world, one sports stadium at a time.

Trevor, I'm so sorry for all the times over the last twenty-eight years that I've fallen painfully short while trying to be the father YOU deserved. And yet I'll always be grateful that, despite all the mistakes I've made, you still find reasons, as undeserved as they may be, to tearfully tell me, "You my hero daddy."

Today, on your birthday, I just want you to know that I'll always love you with all my heart, and with the whole earth as my witness, I would not have traded you or the impact you've had on my life (and on the lives of your mom, brothers, friends and countless others) for anything or with anyone in the world.

That is why I can also finally say that while I still would not consider myself to have been the best choice to be your father, no way, and yet but by the grace of God, the love of our Lord and Savior Jesus Christ, and through the power of the Holy Spirit, I do consider myself, as Trevor's Dad, most richly blessed!

Happy Birthday Trevor! Love, Dad

Robert Hendershot

Sweet Caroline and Burger King

Lynn Martin Burkett

"Down syndrome isn't a burden; how people react to it is."

My new favorite quote sums up a lot after living for sixteen years with a daughter with Down syndrome. I can go many days or weeks without Down syndrome being an issue for me. It's the rest of the world that just doesn't quite get it, but I think the world is changing for the better and is becoming more inclusive and accepting of people with disabilities.

We have always pushed Caroline to try hard and enrolled her in activities that would put her in close proximity to other children without disabilities, such as Girl Scouts, Tee Ball, Upward basketball, and soccer and dance classes. And, of course, general education classes. We have been blessed with some great teachers throughout her school career. The best teachers are the ones who are accepting of Caroline's limitations and do not get exasperated by her.

To me, there is nothing more important than inclusion. My husband and I have always believed Caroline would work with non-disabled peers, so they needed to be exposed to her as much as she needed to be exposed to them. Modeling her non-disabled peers has been more helpful than any type of therapy. As she progresses through her school career, we have become more focused on letting her enjoy school and all of its social aspects and less focused on making the honor roll. Caroline's diploma is not going to necessarily open or close any doors for her. Her disability cannot be "hidden," and she will be hired only if she can fulfill the job requirements.

Caroline turning sixteen and successfully obtaining her first job as a "Greetings Ambassador" at Burger King has confirmed our beliefs that inclusion works. Caroline wants to be included in all aspects of her life and she has now accomplished this in school and in her employment. She dreams of attending a two-year LIFE college program and saves all of her paychecks to help pay for college. We cannot wait to see what the future holds for our Sweet Caroline.

Lynn Martin Burkett, is a mom to one daughter with Down syndrome and two younger brothers. They live in Marion, VA, and enjoy the small-town life.

Yes, I'm "THAT" Mom

Pamela R. Meeks

My daughter is currently a junior in high school and for the most part has been fully included. I'm not going to say the road has been easy, but it has not been completely difficult either. We've seen good times and we have seen our daughter thrive among her peers. We have seen her grow academically as well as socially. In our case, inclusion has been a key component to this growth.

We have advocated since preschool—sometimes quite strongly—for my daughter to be fully included. In kindergarten, the special education teacher greeted our daughter with the message that she would be in the resource room a few hours each day. We made it clear immediately that was not happening. (We were in a three-hour kindergarten class—let's get real—clearly that didn't happen.) This actually turned into a very healthy relationship, one of respect as well as give and take.

I certainly have the title of "that mom" and I'm okay with that. We try to keep the focus on advocacy and not fighting.

We were known and respected in our school. We had and continue to have a positive relationship with most teachers and staff. When presented with a problem, we approached it professionally and often used it as a teaching opportunity. We know our rights and our daughter's rights and state them firmly but politely. Yes, I probably came across as a Mama Bear at times, but I have also been known to apologize for my attitude after the fact, while still making it clear that the message needed to be heard. I do not think the school or the system were ever out to get us. (Okay, once or twice that may have crossed my mind, lol!). I do believe that their goals and expectations were, at times, different than ours. I believe that sometimes thinking outside of the box was important for all of us.

I have found that the squeaky wheel gets the oil. I don't like being the squeaky wheel, but I occasionally was. As a result, my daughter received the services and supports that she needed, was entitled to, and that were documented in her IEP.

We strive to make sure that the IEP is clear, as sometimes both parties can interpret a single goal, accommodation, or modification differently.

Things happen and there were times we needed to be flexible. As long as that flexibility was a simple speed bump in the road and not a boulder, we rolled with it. We would try to understand where the other side was coming from or that perhaps there was a temporary situation that was out of their control. We found offering a solution or idea to help would help.

We have found that professionalism, respect, compromise, and politeness go a long way. Know the chain of command and try to follow it. When presented with a challenge, pause briefly. Approach it after careful thought and research to remove the emotion from the equation so that the facts (from all perspectives) are fully known and shared. There have been times when I looked at things from the teacher's vantage point and was able to see where they were coming from. Sometimes I compromised a bit, sometimes I didn't. If I wanted my voice heard, I needed to listen to their voice as well.

I realize every student, regardless of ability, is different, has unique goals and unique challenges. Every family is different, and every state and school district are different. I've had to personally keep this in mind when speaking with other families. Their choices may not be our choices, but they are usually right for them. While I may be disappointed by another family's choice, I have to remember that it is theirs to make. I try to pay attention and try to keep in mind that their goals are different, their child is different, and their school/district is different as well.

Communication is key. Develop a rapport with the gen ed teachers and special education teachers. This is a partnership; work together for common ground and acceptable solutions. Make yourself approachable. Don't wait until before the IEP to discover that something has not been followed. At the same time, allow a 'reasonable' time for things to be set in motion (with the exception of safety issues! which must be adhered to all times).

I admit that it greatly saddens me to see the number of children around the country that are being denied the opportunity to have meaningful inclusion and an education alongside their peers. In many cases this is starting in kindergarten and preschool. I realize now that while I have had to advocate strongly, it has not been near the struggle that others have experienced. I have heard some rough statistics recently on inclusion practices and it seems like things have taken a step backward as a whole. I don't have the answers, but encourage those coming along behind me to continue to advocate (not fight). Continue to believe in your son or daughter and yourself. Take care of yourself. Being the parent (and often primary caregiver) of a child with special needs is stressful enough. Adding advocacy creates more stress. Breathe.

Pamela R Meeks is a wife of an amazing husband and mom to two daughters, the youngest of which Rocks an extra chromosome. They live in Colorado and are loving life.

Dear Clueless Teenager

Adrianna McCullar

The man you mocked tonight is my brother, Reuben.

Since you didn't take into account that he is an individual just like you are, let me take this opportunity to teach you a few things about him:

1) My brother LOVES to laugh and, other than baseball, it is his favorite pastime. It is not unusual for him to become interested in other people who are doing what he enjoys: laughing. For this I am grateful, because he didn't even realize you were making fun of him. He sat and smiled his handsome smile and paid your behavior no attention whatsoever.

2) Reuben is pretty much a self-declared local celebrity. Everywhere we go, he's waving and smiling, and folks go out of their way to greet him. This is not because he is rich or has a lot of followers on Instagram. It's because he spreads happiness and joy wherever he goes, and people love him for it. Had you taken the time, I feel certain you would've seen this too.

3) The crown he was wearing tonight was from Tim Tebow's Night to Shine Prom. And while it may not mean anything to you, the crown reminded me, as his sister, that Reuben is celebrated and valued by an army of people. These same people see past a label and a disability into the heart of who he IS, a child of God.

So my dear, the point of my story is this: I am going to pray for you tonight.

I am going to pray that one day your heart is touched by someone with special needs. I am going to pray that if you become a parent, you won't ever have to sit and listen to a doctor or specialist tell you all of the things your child won't be able to do because of a diagnosis or disability. But mostly I am going to pray that you heard me when I said, "Don't worry Rube, she just doesn't realize how awesome you are."

Because you didn't get it, you are going to miss out on a lot of fantastic people with an attitude like that.

Regardless, I am going to sleep tonight grateful that I got to boogie down with some awesome dancers, moved that so many in our community of Lexington made such an event possible and blessed that we are currently watching *Home Alone 2* for the fourteenth million time with The World's Coolest Brother.

My hope is that someone shares this post so that somewhere out there an adult will have an educated conversation with their child, sibling, niece, nephew, or friend about accepting and understanding those with special needs. I think if you could ask every person who attended tonight's prom, they'd be able to share something interesting they learned about their buddy tonight.

We all have more in common than you might think.

Adrianna McCullar lives in Lexington, SC, where she runs and operates an early interventions agency for kids with special needs. Her brother, Reuben, is the Happiness Coordinator at Carolina Behavior and Beyond.

The Ripple Effect of Inclusion

Jessica Crain

As a kid, I did not know one person with Down syndrome, not one person. By the time I was an adult, I had had zero
interactions with a person with Down syndrome. I had heard about Down syndrome, but I had no idea what it was or what it meant. My son was the first person I knew with Down syndrome.

During my son's first week of kindergarten, I nervously went into his classroom to talk about Down syndrome and how he may do some things differently, but most importantly I wanted his class to understand how he was more like them than he was different. Those kindergarteners showed me that day, and every day since, that they see my son as a friend. Plain and simple.

When kids grow up understanding differences are something to be celebrated and that we are all more alike than different, they are less likely to fear people who are different from them. Less fear equals more acceptance and inclusion for all. Down syndrome isn't something that prevents a meaningful life. In fact, I'd argue that Down syndrome makes life more meaningful. I know it has for my family.

Imagine a hospital room where parents of a newborn baby with the most adorable smile and squishy arms and legs have just received a diagnosis of Down syndrome. The father of the baby immediately thinks about his friend from school who also had Down syndrome. He remembers he was kind, worked hard, had the best sense of humor, and loved to make his friends laugh. He says to his wife, "Our little boy is going to be great; he is something to celebrate! We are lucky to have him in our lives." Those parents will have a positive connection and believe in their son and raise him with high expectations and a lot of love.

This is the ripple effect of inclusion. If a peer in my son's class has a child with Down syndrome in the future, they will remember my son and see their baby as capable and a gift. My son is helping to change the future of the world just by working hard and teaching his peers that Down syndrome isn't something to be feared. Differences are a beautiful part of life, and all individuals have their own unique talents and gifts.

When we first started on our inclusion journey, we wanted inclusion for our son because we knew it was best for him. I also knew it would be beneficial for his peers, but I didn't understand the magnitude of what my son was doing to help change the world by shaping his peers' perceptions. Many times this year I have seen his classmates show kindness, empathy, and understanding. They naturally slow their pace to accommodate his slower pace. They talk to him same as they do all their other friends, regardless of how he responds. They help and include him.

Inclusion is truly a win-win. When my son started the school year, he was unsure of his abilities. Recently, he read his sight words in front of his class, loud and clear. This accomplishment is the result of increased self-confidence, pride in his work and that he feels included in his class. The more confident individuals with Down syndrome are, the more likely they will be to engage with their community and share their full potential.

A truly inclusive world in the future begins with more inclusive experiences now. Inclusion creates a ripple effect that benefits not only the person being included, but also shapes the perceptions of their peers, now and in the future-which can change cultural perceptions. When we start viewing differences as unique gifts, a truly inclusive world is possible.

Jessica Crain is a contributor to The Mighty and shares her family's inclusive education experience on her blog.

Devin Belongs

Gena Mitchell

From the beginning, Devin's pre-school IEP team suggested that she go to a learning center for kindergarten rather than to our neighborhood school with her sisters. Ironically, they believed a great deal in her abilities, but she was a runner and considered a "flight risk," so their focus was safety. Thankfully, after a three-plus-hour meeting and a great deal of discussion, she would be attending elementary school with her sisters in an inclusive kindergarten class along with a 1:1 para educator.

It's been ten years since that meeting and Devin has been in an inclusive classroom through her freshman year in high school.

Some years have been great, others not so much. Some teachers have been amazing; others, let's just say *"eh, could have been better."* But the reality is that that has happened for all of my three girls, not just to the one who has Down syndrome. Devin is a part of her school and our community, just like her sisters, her classmates, and our neighbors. THAT is what I thought about going into that IEP meeting so many years ago, and THAT is the guiding star we have followed to make decisions for Devin year after year after year.

I think it would be unfair to paint a picture of unicorns and rainbows, because it hasn't always been pretty and sweet. I have received the calls about an incident or attended meetings about her behavior. Once, she slammed a door and, of course, it was directly on a classmate's hand. She has struggled with concepts that come easily to her classmates. She didn't stay at the same pace with reading and she would plateau for great lengths of time in certain subjects. If we had looked at each of these academic pieces individually or even collectively but without the whole picture of who she is, it could have made a case for a self-contained classroom or maybe a different program. But Devin's whole picture has never been solely about math problems, science experiments, or always cutting a straight line. Devin succeeds daily in overcoming obstacles, so to focus on one area and limit her is something our family has never subscribed to.

From standing in line for recess, to waiting her turn, to manipulating her locker, to completing sequenced tasks, to walking the halls to class of a 2000+ person school independently, inclusion has given Devin peers to model at every turn. I don't mean that she has learned everything she needs to know from her peers, but "on the job training" has a lasting impression. That's what inclusion is for: this job called life. And if the reality of the other students in the class is to have someone with Down syndrome, or another disability, in it, then that becomes their perceived reality of life and this will hopefully carry over even outside of the classroom.

When Devin was going into second grade, I saw a mom who told me that her son asked if he was in Devin's class for the upcoming year. When she told him no, not this year, he was really disappointed. To her it was just a passing conversation. To me, it was validation that Devin was viewed as a classmate and a valued part of their school. It was Devin's class he wanted to be in. She wasn't an outsider, being tolerated because she needed help, and everyone needed to be nice to her—she belonged! In middle school, I heard about an issue at school from a couple of moms because their kids were worried about Devin. They didn't think she should have been getting into trouble and it turned out they were right. These students spoke up for Devin when she couldn't. They looked out for her—that is belonging!

In high school, Devin asked to try out for the cheerleading team. She ended up making the JV squad and she is now cheering for those same kids on the football field and basketball court. She sees these kids and many more at the store, the movies, museums, restaurants, and so many other places. I have strangers come up and introduce themselves and say, "Are you Devin's mom?" or "I see her at

Whitman," or "I see her cheer," or "my son/daughter was in her class."

I believe inclusion is Devin being a part of her school and community. It is her teammates walking with her from class to practice at the end of the day. It is eating lunch with her friends outside on the sidewalk on a sunny day. It is her working in a small group in her astronomy class on an experiment or taking a test that the teacher has modified for her to complete independently.

Inclusion: don't get caught up in those nine letters, make it bigger. Seek inclusion for what it means for your son or daughter as part of their school and community.

Love inclusion for what it is: belonging. It's an amazing gift to give your child.

Gena Mitchell is a mother, advocate for all individuals with disabilities, a small business owner, and non-profit founder. She lives in Maryland with her husband; three daughters, one of whom has Down syndrome; and their two yellow labs.

"We should assume that poor performance is due to instructional inadequacy rather than to student deficit; in other words, if a student does not do well, the quality of the instructions should be questioned before the student's ability to learn"
~ Donnell 1984

"Inclusion is not a strategy to help people fit into the systems and structures which exist in our societies; it is about transforming those systems and structures to make it better for everyone."
~ Diane Richler, Past-President, Inclusion International

Why Inclusion is Important

Laura Chapnek

When asked why inclusion is important to me, two things came to my mind.

My first thoughts jump to the time when my son, William, was in kindergarten. He basically had to earn his way into kindergarten and into that gen ed classroom. I feel strongly that all children should start out included in the gen ed class and move from there based on their individual needs.

Secondly, I feel it is very important that all children be able to learn from each other. For the children that are behind their peers, they benefit by observing the other children and having a good example to model. For the children that excel in their grade level, they can in turn help teach the ones that need help or extra time the topic/concepts require. This helps the children that have learned the concept quickly to master the topic/concept by teaching it to others. This works for all people in general, regardless of the situation. It even works in a business model for adults! Why wouldn't we implement this concept for children and also teach empathy, community, and patience at the same time?

One of the truly important things is having the curriculum modified correctly. When the modifications are done correctly and at their level, the children with learning disabilities or different learners, can stay in the best environment/gen ed classroom for a longer time with their peers. If William had had the proper curriculum modifications in middle school, he would have been able to spend more time in the general education classroom. I believe that children who are classified as different learners should have access to a modified curriculum that is approved by the state to coincide with the grade-level curriculum presented to the general education students. This is the true meaning of exposure to the gen ed classroom that many, many of we parents want. Too often these modifications are not well done and the students with learning disabilities are ignored, removed from the gen ed classroom or given busy work to keep them quiet. All students should be challenged and engaged in the topic just as much as their typical peers.

Laura Chapnek has been married for seventeen years and has a fifteen-year-old son with Down syndrome. She serves on the Board of DSNetwork of Arizona and chairs the Phoenix Children's Hospital Fashion Show benefiting the Down Syndrome Clinic. She also does "A Day in the Life" presentations to schools, groups, and civic communities throughout the state of Arizona.

My Heart Broke Today

Heather Hanenburg

My heart broke a little today. I saw you when you squirmed around uncomfortably after my daughter waved and smiled at you. My precious baby loves to make people smile—she's beautiful like that. I saw how hard she kept trying to make you smile. I saw how hard you worked to avoid making eye contact. My beautiful baby is like any other baby; she's more alike than different. She is smart, strong, resilient, and motivated to accomplish anything she sets her mind to. Good things come in threes, like the Holy Trinity. And like her 21st chromosome. I wanted to tell you that Down syndrome is not contagious, but kindness is. I wanted to tell you that my youngest daughter is the most amazing person I've ever known. That she's already been through and overcome more in her seventeen months of life than most people accomplish in fifty years of life. She doesn't care if someone looks a little different. She is pure joy personified and she tries to spread that joy to everyone she meets. She saw you tonight. But she didn't see you the way I did. Because she's better than that. She's better than us. You see, Savannah has made all of us better people. She has made our family realize what is important in life, she has shown us how beautiful real, genuine, unconditional love feels. She has shown us how there is still a lot of beauty left in this world. She is a source of absolute, overwhelming joy. Yet you still worked so hard to not make eye contact with her. You didn't get a glimpse of the love and joy she shares with everyone around her. You missed out on an amazing opportunity with an exceptional young lady. I'm nothing special, but SHE is. I am happier than I have ever been. We all absolutely adore her. The true showing of strength in this life is only 10% what happens to you, because 90% of who you are is based on HOW YOU HANDLE what happens to you. Tonight, a little girl with Down syndrome smiled and waved to you several times. The way you handled that happening to you was incredibly heartbreaking.

Heather Hanenburg is a mom to three; her youngest daughter has DS. They live in Boaz, AL, and are active as a family in the DS community.

A Valued Part of the Community

Michelle Tetschner

It was morning. I had just walked my son into our school and was turning to go to my car. Suddenly, another mom waved to me across the parking lot. While I didn't know her personally, I did recognize her as a mom of a younger child. I didn't know her well, as she has children younger than my seventh grader, and we were new to the school.

As I walked up to her, she seemed very emotional. I stopped immediately, ready to help.

She excitedly said, "My son is in fourth grade with the other new little boy who has Downs!

I am so excited for the life lessons my child is going to learn in this classroom with him in it!

Us moms were texting yesterday—did you see the adorable little special boy who's in our kids' class? and we are all so excited!" She teared up and gave me a big hug and turned quickly away.

She got it.

She understood that my son and this other little boy will teach amazing things to these other children!

I stood there for a moment, caught off guard. I was expecting to help her, but she had completely given ME a gift.

A gift of acceptance. A gift of understanding the gifts my son truly has.

While the words weren't politically correct and the language wasn't people first, the sentiment was overwhelmingly correct.

I love it when people truly "get it!!"

Michelle Tetschner 2017

26 Firsts Achieved by People with Down Syndrome

Sandra McElwee

The first registered Capitol Hill lobbyist with Down syndrome, *Kayla McKeon*, 30, who works for the National Down Syndrome Society, has already helped achieve *passage* of the ABLE to Work Act, 2018.

Jamie Brewer is one of our superstars and is paving the way for so many with Down syndrome. In February 2018, she became the *first woman with DS to star in an Off-Broadway play, Amy and the Orphans*. In June, she was the first actor with Down syndrome to win a Drama Desk award and she won it for *Outstanding Featured Actress in a Play*. Again breaking another barrier, Jamie debuted as the *first runway model with DS in New York's Fashion Week* in February 2015, modeling an original design by Carrie Hammer.

First Gerber Spokesbaby with DS, Lucas Warren, February 2018. Gerber started the Spokesbaby program 91 years ago.

In 2017, Hanna Atkinson and Connor Long became the first-ever people with IDD/DS to earn *personal Emmys* for their work as contributing broadcast news reporters. And in 2016, they became the first ever *news reporters* with Down syndrome.

November 2017, Mikayla Holgren became the first woman with DS to compete in a *Miss USA State Pageant*, where she was awarded the Spirit of Miss USA and the Director's Award. She then went on to win the very first ever *Miss Congeniality at the Global Beauty Awards* in Seattle in March 2018.

Born This Way was the first television show featuring an ensemble cast of people with Down syndrome to win an Emmy for *Outstanding Unstructured Reality Program.*

After battling for years for the right to compete, *Garett "G-Money" Holeve* finally realized his dream of fighting in a sanctioned MMA match in October 2015.

June 2015,*Marcus Sikora published* the first children's book written by a person with DS, *Black Day: The Monster Rock Band.*

December 2014, Ezra Roy, 26, graduated *magna cum laude* with a *Bachelor of Fine Arts from TSU.*

May 2013, Jimmy Jenson, 48, was the first man with Down syndrome to complete the *New York Marathon* in a little over eight hours, encouraging everyone he passed along the way to keep going.

Karen Gaffney was the first to receive an honorary doctorate degree from the University of Portland in May 2013. But she's broken more records than that. Widely known for her other firsts in 2001, completion or swimming a relay across the English Channel, and her 2007 swim across Lake Tahoe.

In May 2013, Megan McCormick was the first person in the United States with Down syndrome to graduate with *honors from a technical college*, Bluegrass Community and Technical College.

Yulissa Arescurenaga is the *first certified Zumba instructor* with Down syndrome, receiving her certificate in 2012.

Chelsea Warner was the first person with DS to *compete in USA Gymnastics* in 2008.

January 1996, Sandra Jensen was the first woman with DS to *receive an organ transplant*. Still today, states deny organ transplants to people with DS and other intellectual disabilities and the NDSS is fighting for their rights to medical care.

In 1987, Judith Scott was introduced to fiber art and became famous for her sculptures. She was the *first artist with Down syndrome whose art was featured in art galleries—many galleries.*

In 1994, Jason Kingsley and Mitchell Levitz published the *first autobiographical book* by adults with Down syndrome, "Count Us In."

In 1989. Chris Burke became the first major character with DS on a *prime-time television show.*

They say when you break a glass ceiling you will get slivers.

Sandra McElwee, is the author of three books about her son, Sean, and is the Chief Dream Facilitator supporting his T-shirt design business and website at Seanese.com.

Brandon Says Labels Are for Cans, Not People!

Tim Gruber

Imagine your child went through three years of middle school, earning honor roll or honor society every quarter, then moving to a new school district shortly thereafter to begin high school. If you were like my wife and me, we were excited about our son's prospects, given his academic prowess and proven track record. On top of this, he was to attend the same high school where we met, fell in love, and were star athletes. It appeared the table was made to order and laid out perfectly for the next part of the academic journey. Visions of grandeur where clubs were easy to access and become a part of. Where prom was no longer a far-off fantasy, but one close at hand and wildly anticipated. Continuing to take part in school plays where his unique talents could continue to develop and shine. And lastly, enjoying high school dances were images etched deeply into our being.

Then something was lost in translation. His transcripts were dismissed because his diagnosis of Down syndrome held more weight in the school's eyes than his prior performance. Clubs were not an option because he wasn't viewed as a regular student. Drama was another door left locked for reasons still not understood. We also learned that accessing homecoming was for everyone except our son and a few others identified as "special education" students. In two short months, we had gone from king of the hill, an A student, full inclusion to the opposite. The explanation, "he has Down syndrome, so whatever he did prior to high school is inconsequential and inflated." This was the first time during his academic journey where we were sorted by a label with no regard for the person outside the diagnosis.

As my wife and I planned, plotted, and navigated our next steps, our son, Brandon, used the challenges as motivation to change the fiber of the school. When homecoming came around and he wanted to be part of the parade and float, he didn't ask for permission to join. He showed up, rolled up his sleeves, and demonstrated top-tier school spirit. When he was initially placed into the "special education" classes and forced to eat lunch at a certain table, he removed himself and headed to the senior quad where he mingled with the entire student population. Yes, the calls came from administrators and so-called case managers that this wasn't part of the program, their calls did nothing to dissuade Brandon from his goals. Eventually, hearts and minds began to change when, as a freshman, he made the boys basketball team. The tide was slowly ebbing in his favor. He now had the best athletes in his class on his side who saw he was capable, and more importantly, a great teammate.

There was a point during the struggle where we were looking to remove him from the high school midway through his junior year when drama, access to certain classes, and his application for ASB were denied. He had other plans and told us "they haven't seen the real me and I want to show them that I am capable of many things." We quickly realized that Brandon had turned a life-changing corner on his road to independence and self-determination. We agreed to let him do it his way, and what happened in a span of twelve months can only be described as epic.

He applied once again to become part of ASB Leadership because he knew this was where the students of influence resided. When his initial attempt to get in was denied, he advocated on his behalf to get an interview. He got the interview and was selected as part of ASB. Next up was inclusion in a campus club. He decided the best place for him to earn acceptance without label was the Migrant Student Association (MSA). This club was a safe haven for Mexican-American students on campus, and although Brandon is not Hispanic, he was accepted with open arms. He soon earned the surname of Santiago Chavez and proudly wore his Mexican national team jersey to club meetings.

On a Tuesday in mid-September, I received a call from my wife reluctantly informing me that Brandon was nominated for the Homecoming court. This didn't seem plausible given his experiences the prior three years, so we had to verify for accuracy. Sure enough, he was on the ballot along with fifteen other seniors. From this, five would be selected to be part of the court and one eventually the king. A week later votes were cast, and Brandon informed us he was in the final five. We were elated for him because this was one of his dreams entering high school, but also unsure of the final outcome, which could be another disappointment. But we were overjoyed with him becoming a prince. Then homecoming arrived in late September, and we were dressed to the nines because parents and the court had to go on the field at halftime of the football game where the king and queen would be announced. As the hours turned to minutes, the voice from the loudspeaker resonated for all to hear "this year's homecoming king is Brandon Gruber." The only one not surprised by the victory was Brandon. He was so confident that he would become king that when he stood and waved to the crowd, it was if he were taking a leisurely walk through the park. It felt surreal to see the smile on his face and a crowd so caught up in the moment. The lights, cameras, cheering, hugging, and crisp fall air all melted into a pictorial viewed at warp speed. He had advocated and won on his own terms.

What followed over the course of his final year was born on this glorious day. He was voted "Best Dancer and Most School Spirit," earned all A's, and he started a foundation where he sold his art cards to help send many of his MSA brethren to prom and winter formals, as well as provide yearbooks for other students without the financial means to buy their own. He appeared in *People* magazine on two separate occasions for his philanthropy and inspirational journey.

The boy had become a man and, therefore, the man didn't allow the struggle to defeat him.

He beat the system, altered minds, and knocked down locked doors. The convergence of will and hard work on his part re-engineered the game and laid a foundation for other uniquely qualified individuals: a roadmap to follow.

Brandon tells my wife and me all the time that "labels are for cans, not people." This is why he never accepted the status quo. He wanted more and thus set goals that not only seemed improbable but appeared impossible. He lives by a simple motto that drives him every day of his life: work hard, choose kindness every day, and be yourself.

We know Brandon's journey is far from complete and struggles loom before us that we have yet to encounter. We remain ardent in our support of his artistic and college goals, and his past has made it clear no mountain is too high for him to climb as long as he continues to dream big and embrace the struggle.

Tim Gruber is a husband to Teresa (Super Mom) and father to Brandon (22), who finds inspiration each day by watching his son break down barriers every step along the way.

We Can't All Be a CEO

Lois Matti

What kind of world would we have if everyone wanted to be a president and CEO? Who would do the essential work that needs to be done day in and day out that makes our world function? Every job is essential, just as every person doing those jobs is essential, and in this 21st century every person should have the opportunity to learn, train, and do the work that most inspires them. So why do we continually encounter those who want to place students and workers in a segregated box? Is it because that is where they belong or because it is easier for the teachers, supervisors, and employers?

My godson has Down syndrome, and I am continually inspired by his zest for life, his willingness to love and give unconditionally, and his desire to try new things and take new adventures. In fact, his mind and willingness are more open than many of my typical friends and work colleagues. If they had this attitude, we would encourage them to grow, expand and discover new opportunities. Shouldn't we also do this for our family, friends, and colleagues with intellectual disabilities?

When I talk to him about school, he tells me about his friends that support and encourage him to learn and play right alongside them. He shares his love of music that is encouraged when he is included in choir and when he earns a role in the school musical. His can-do attitude is greater than many of the typical children of other friends and family that I know. And when I have gone to his school, I see that his friends genuinely want him to be with them as a peer, a friend, and fellow participant. These students are our future doctors, lawyers, and leaders in our communities. Being equipped with the opportunity to fully understand everyone where they are in life, will make them more inclusive members and leaders in our society.

Do we really want to be so small minded that we think that because of perceived intellectual abilities that we should limit whether a person can learn to read, write, or work? In this age of innovation, let's not leave behind or try to limit what those with an intellectual disability can do. If we only look at our past, we are not going to create the new and better future we all want for us and our children.

~~~~~~

Lois Matti is mom to two beautiful daughters, lives in Minnesota, and is passionate that people with disabilities have gifts and strengths that just need to be discovered.

Fellow Classmates
FIRE Foundation

I have learned to accept every person, not just those with special needs. Having an individual with Down syndrome in my class has opened my eyes and made me realize that including people with disabilities not only helps that person, but also the entire grade. When my classmates and I interact with him, it makes us feel happy to know that he is enjoying school and being treated exactly like any other student. He would not be included in everyday activities if he were not part of the Foundation for Inclusive Religious Education (FIRE) program. He enables me to have a positive outlook every day. His happiness ripples through our school and is contagious. Having him as a classmate has positively impacted our grade and shown us all how to make the most of life.

Without the FIRE program, I would never have met him. In our friendship, he has certainly taught me more than I have him; he teaches me to be a better person—to be accepting of all people, no matter their abilities, and to live like Christ. Some folks don't learn this lesson in a lifetime; but because of the FIRE program, I can grasp this first hand. I know we are all simply called to love and accept everyone.

The FIRE program is one that has helped me learn the importance of being thankful, patient, kind, and respectful. Without their helping hands in my school and heart, I would be a much different person. I am able to persevere through tough situations, understand that we all have special gifts, and appreciate the wonderful gifts God has given us.

No matter how dire a situation may seem, there is always a way to get through it. He lights up my day because of his ability to stay positive. Through FIRE, I was able to learn that one of the best gifts God can give us is the gift of being different.

With the determination and compassion FIRE students have conveyed to me, I know that no challenge can hold me back. I can help others by being compassionate towards them.

Through FIRE, I have realized that helping others reach their full potential is something that I can and love to do. Just by being some-one who smiles when someone is having a hard time or helping them understand how to do a problem, I can be a positive influence on others. The opportunity to be a part of a school who participates in FIRE has been one of the best of my life and will always help me in the future with my patience, kindness, and my overall relation-ship with God. I know I can and will carry on the foundation of Christ's attitude FIRE has instilled in me.

I watch my mom struggle daily to communicate. I watch people turn away, make faces, and say unkind things about my mom. I am new to Our Lady of Hope this year and I have to tell you it's been the best thing that ever happened to me. When I first met this stu-dent, I knew I wanted to help her so that she would not feel ashamed or embarrassed due to her disability. Every day she struggles at school to make herself understood. I am there for her every day to help and support. I want my classmates to see that it's easy to step up, not judge, and be a support for others

---

I have learned to accept every person, not just those with special needs. Having an individual with Down syndrome in my class has opened my eyes and made me realize that including people with disabilities not only helps that person, but also the entire grade.

When my classmates and I interact with him, it makes us feel happy to know that he is enjoying school and being treated exactly like any other student. He would not be included in everyday activities if he were not part of the FIRE program.

He enables me to have a positive outlook every day. His happiness ripples through our school and is contagious. Having him as a class-mate has positively impacted our grade and shown us all how to make the most of life. Without the FIRE program, I would never have met him. In our friendship, he has certainly taught me more than I have him; he teaches me to be a better person—to be accepting of all people, no matter their abilities, and to live like Christ. Some folks don't learn this lesson in a lifetime; but because of the FIRE program, I can grasp this first hand. I know we are all simply called to love and accept everyone.

Stories contributed by FIRE of Kansas City. Every year students attending schools in the Diocese of Kansas City-St. Joseph submit essays that provide a brief glimpse into their hearts. Through their words, we hear the voices of our most passionate inclusion advocates. Through these young people's experiences and through the friendships they have formed, the call to include all students, of all abilities, rings loud and clear - Lynn Hire executive director.

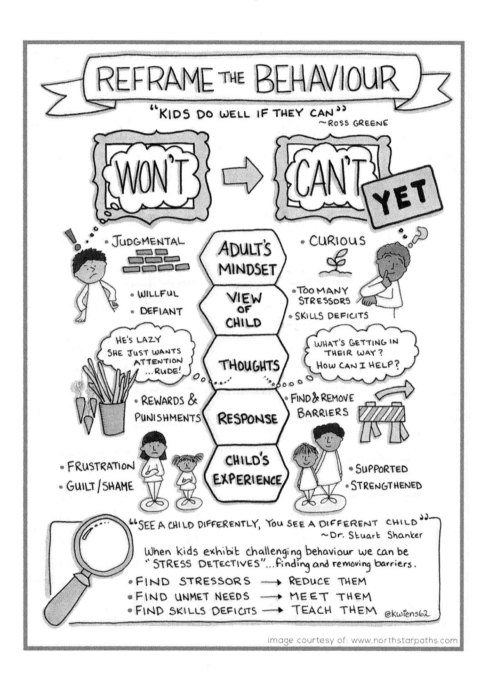

Treated As Equals

Kenna Cassey

Kids with disabilities such as autism and Down syndrome are often outcasted in schools and in society. In some schools, students with disabilities are pushed to the farthest corners of the campus. But not here.

Since it opened in 2007, the school has made a concerted effort to include its special needs students into classes or clubs where they are treated as equals to the typical students.

Senior Fletcher Jones is in student council and junior Alyssa Uzueta is in culinary. These students are in regular classes just like many other kids where they are treated as equals. They have had to adapt to a new environment, but special needs students like them fit right in here on campus. Uzueta is a ray of sunshine right when she enters the door to culinary class. She always has a huge smile on her face and is open to learning new things. She has made new friends and enjoys getting to learn new life skills. As teacher Mrs. Albornoz says, "I enjoy it because by the end of the year I get to see these kids improve life skills."

Jones is always at his happiest when he gets to go to student council. He has made many new friends and enjoys receiving the spotlight student council brings to him. Jones' student council teacher Lerina Johnson said, "I look at inclusion as one race, and it is a human race, and that the more we can do to include everyone a better place Perry high school is."

Jones is included in many school activities outside of the classroom. Alongside STUGO, he has been part of the drama department plays, Puma Pals, and unified sports.

These students are included by some people, but others are not as accepting. Just because they are unique does not mean that they do not have feelings or basic emotions. Just because they are different doesn't mean that they are no longer human. Just because they do not react when people are picking on them does not mean that they do not know when they are being picked on. The kids are smart if not smarter than typical students. The kids have things that they are passionate about just like any regular student. They have interests just like a typical student. These kids have feelings and want to be accepted in society just like anyone else does.

Kenna Cassey is a student at Perry High School. Kenna was named 2017 Buddy of the Year, western region. She volunteers her time to TopSoccer, Puma Pals, and Unified sports.

Windows Into Heaven

Stacy and Michelle Tetschner

After 12 years of marriage, we were living a blessed life with two happy, healthy sons. We weren't planning on expanding our family, either naturally or through adoption, at this time. But fate intervened, and we became aware of a baby girl who needed some loving care. Her parents were experiencing a series of struggles, forcing them to send her to live with relatives who are no longer able to care for her. We could not bear to see this beautiful baby girl go into the foster care system, so we agreed to take her into our home. Within six weeks, the baby's parents worked out their problems and she returned home. Her departure left an emotional void that prompted us to become a licensed foster family. We looked forward to providing a home filled with love to children who needed extra help.

Over the next nine months, we attended classes and learned about things that should never happen to children and yet they do. Our home was scrutinized and inspected to ensure a safe environment for any child who came to live with us. We educated ourselves about potential challenges. It was not an easy process. Occasionally, we would ask ourselves if it was really worth it. Instinctively, however, we knew that to become licensed foster parents was our calling and we focused on fulfilling the requirements. At the same time there was another little soul who was facing his own challenges. His mother had faced many obstacles throughout her life that prevented her from being the best mom she could for the children she already had. Four weeks before her due date, she delivered a 5 pound baby boy who had another challenge to her complicated life: he had Down syndrome.

Our lives synchronized one Tuesday morning when Michelle was grocery shopping. She received a call from Melissa, our foster placement worker who asked if we were ready for our first placement. Melissa described a five-day-old Native American boy who had Down syndrome and needed an emergency placement for 2 to 3 weeks. A few days earlier, his mother had left the hospital without him. Michelle jotted down all the details about this baby boy and, after talking to Melissa, she called me about helping this little boy for the next 2 to 3 weeks.

When Michelle was pregnant with our biological children, we discussed Down syndrome and how to prepare for it; however, our foster parenting classes did not cover special-needs training. Nonetheless, we thought we could meet this challenge to provide a loving home for this baby, until an adoptive family was found.

At 10:30 a.m. Michelle called Melissa back to let her know we agreed to take him into our home. Melissa informed us that we needed to pick the baby up at the hospital by 1:00 p.m.! That gave us less than three hours to prepare for what took nine months to do the last time. Michelle made a quick U-turn from the checkout line, and went back to the baby department to load up on all the necessary supplies.

Giving birth to your own child and taking him or her home from the hospital is an amazing experience, but going to the hospital to pick up an infant that we did not give birth to was surreal. After finding the hospitals NICU ward, we were introduced to a little peanut of a baby named Raymond, who weighed barely 5 pounds. He had jet black hair and the face of an angel.

The nurses were just completing his medical test, and it seemed we should be ready to leave soon. The discharge process seem to drag on and after 90 minutes we finally asked the nurse how soon we would be able to take Raymond home. Curtly she stated, "I will let you take MY baby home when I am ready."

Later, we learned that this nurse had been working 12 hour shifts for three straight days since Raymond's birth. She had to come to be quite protective of this little boy, who was abandoned by his mother. Amazingly, Raymond was touching lives and hearts at barely 5 days old. We left an hour later with Raymond after receiving very detailed instructions regarding his care.

The next three weeks stretched into months as the state of Arizona work through various processes and steps to legally prepare Raymond for adoption. There were court cases and appearances, visits from a variety of people, and mountains of i's to dot and t's to cross. We did not mind the red tape, as our entire family adored Raymond right from the start.

As Raymond grew and became more aware of his surroundings, we noticed his special gift. He could sense when people needed special attention. A visit to the grocery store with him in the cart sparked at least one or two random hugs from a cashier or another customer. Frequently, they responded by remarking how much they needed a hug that day and some would even tear up. Raymond became a little window into heaven for many people everywhere we went.

The three week placement turned into seven months before Raymond was ready to be placed for adoption. When the social worker assigned to his case phoned to introduce herself, she immediately asked Michelle, "So, what's wrong with this baby anyway?"

Although our family tried to maintain some distance in our relationship with Raymond because we wanted to minimize our heart break when he left us, Michelle was infuriated by the social worker's tactless and heartless question, and she did not mince any words telling her that Raymond was perfect, just as God had made him. After Michelle's long-winded response, the social worker paused and asked in the kindest voice, " Then why aren't you adopting him?".

In my profession, I have worked with many outstanding sales people and sales trainers and this, by far, is the best sales technique I have ever heard. We had not considered adoption believing that "God had placed him with us for a little while until the right forever family who needed him was identified." Soon, our family realized that we were the one's who needed him. When we told our boys that we were the right family for Raymond, they said, "Well duh, we are already knew that; it just took you two longer to figure it out "

On National Adoption Day 2003, Raymond became a permanent part of our family. We celebrated with almost 100 people in our backyard, all of whom supported us through this entire process and can tell you that Raymond has shown them a window into heaven. Raymond, wearing a tuxedo, hammed it up all day long. By having Raymond in our family, we have been introduced to incredible people who inspired us to write this book and share a small sampling of inspirational stories revealing how children and adults with Down syndrome are positively changing lives every day.

The title, Windows Into Heaven, has special meaning. When Glenna Salsbury, a professional speaker from Paradise Valley Arizona, addressed our Sharing Down syndrome Arizona group in January 2004, she shared some compelling information about a belief held by a number of Native American tribes. Through their sheer simplicity, children with Down syndrome are believed to be a window to the Great Spirit.

We translated that belief into the title for this book because we feel these children are truly a window into heaven. Whether you are a parent of a child with Down syndrome, are blessed to know someone with Down syndrome, or are just looking for some amazing and inspiring stories, we hope you will look through these windows for a glimpse of heaven that so many of us already know.

~~~~~~

Stacy and Michelle Tetschner are huge advocates for inclusion! They are proud parents of Raymond who is an amazingly funny, talented kid who just wants to belong and be included. This story is as written for the introduction story from their book Windows Into Heaven published in 2008.

Section 2: Inspiring Catholic Stories

A Sense of Belongingness
for all of Gods children

Dr. Marco Clark

Throughout my 30 years in Catholic education, I have often taken leaps of faith to initiate new programs and to manage change. Bishop McNamara High School has experienced tremendous growth and change over its 50 year history including going from an all-male school to coeducational, and having grown from just 200 students in 1992 to now nearly 900 students with a long waiting list. Part of that growth has been embracing the changing demographics of the our region, meeting all students where they are, and creating a welcoming Catholic school environment.

At a School that celebrates its wonderful racial, ethnic, religious and socio-economic diversity, we also recognized that we were not completely fulfilling our call to teach all of God's children because we had not been intentional about opening our doors to students who learn differently. When we created the St. Joseph Program for students with learning differences and then later the St. Andre Program for students with developmental and intellectual disabilities, we took that same leap of faith and began welcoming a new group of students. As a Catholic school in the Holy Cross tradition, we are committed to meeting students where they are. We approach each day with the zeal to make God known, loved and served. And we accept the challenge to form empowered leaders, inspired by the Gospel, who transform the world. By accepting students into our St. Joseph and St. Andre programs, little did we know how we would be transformed as a School, starting with each of us.

As Holy Cross educators we understand that we learn as much from our students as they learn from us and from one another. That could not have been more evident then when we began welcoming students into these programs. I recall one of our first graduates of the St. Joseph Program who proudly walked across the altar at the National Shrine of the Immaculate Conception in Washington D.C., the largest Catholic church in the country, to receive his diploma. As instructed, he received his diploma in his left hand and then shook my hand with his right. He then proceeded to embrace me in a lasting hug as our faculty and staff along with the 3,500 guests in the audience stood to applause him. That embrace felt like it went on for a lifetime. Little did this young man know, but that embrace also signified for all of us that we had gone from creating a welcoming environment for all students to one of belonging.

Since that time, we have seen students from our programs participate fully in the life of the school as leaders in student council, actors and actresses in our plays, musicians, athletes, artists, peer mentors and so much more. Many have gone on to prestigious colleges and universities to be recognized with top graduation awards, including our 2018 award winners of the Holy Cross Award, Cardinal's Award, and the top award we give to a male graduate, the Man of the Year. These programs and the students who have attended our school as a result have made our school better. Blessed Basile Moreau, C.S.C., Founder of the Congregation of Holy Cross, stated, "Education is the art of bringing young people to completeness." By welcoming students who possess various gifts and needs, we have become a more "complete" Catholic school. I am inspired every day by the commitment to the Christian life that is demonstrated by the faculty, staff, parents and students who welcome and create a sense of belongingness for all of God's children.

Dr. Marco Clark has worked as a Catholic educator in the Archdiocese of Washington since 1989. He is a 1985 graduate of Bishop McNamara High School, where he currently serves as the President/CEO. In 2015 Marco received his Doctorate in Education in Interdisciplinary Leadership from Creighton University. He is a member of the Leadership Advisory Council for the NCEA. In 2012 he was awarded the Secondary Schools' Administrator of the Year Award from the National Catholic Educational Association. He is married to Peggy Clark, also a Catholic school teacher, and has three children and two grandchildren. They reside in the Town of Cheverly, MD.

A Win-Win For All

Katie Carden

After making his entrance into the world, my youngest son received a diagnosis of Down syndrome. I was reassured by the great possibilities children like Ryan would have and how far society has come in terms of acceptance. I was at the same time, paralyzed by the fact that the doors to Catholic education would likely be closed to him. This thought haunted me during his early years as I watched my other five children flourish in Catholic schools. Being both a parent and Catholic school principal has given me a unique perspective on inclusion in our Catholic schools.

During Ryan's first year of life, I began to see a transformation in his siblings. Each of them, unique in their own way, was beginning to share some common character traits: patience, tolerance, compassion, empathy, acceptance and a desire to advocate for the marginalized. These traits were regularly recognized by teachers, coaches and parents – and like the seeds of a dandelion, began to spread to their classmates, friends and teammates.

As I experienced inclusion firsthand as a win-win for all, I wrestled with some tough questions. Were students with disabilities being shortchanged from the lack of opportunity to learn and grow in faith alongside their typical developing peers? Were typical developing students in our Catholic school system being shortchanged by the lack of opportunity to learn alongside the marginalized?

Loyola University (Chicago) apparently shared my vision, and finding them was an answer to my prayers. I became passionate and hopeful about the possibilities after attending their annual Mustard Seed Conference that advocated for serving students with disabilities in Catholic school settings. Here, like-minded educators further ignited my passion for Catholic school inclusion, and I enrolled in the first cohort of the "All are Welcome Program" (Loyola University), designed to support Catholic school principals in innovative ways to implement inclusive practices and open their doors to the marginalized.

Armed with knowledge, I set to work to open the minds of stakeholders—teachers, parents, board members and students—to the responsibility, possibilities and benefits of inclusion. And in October 2016, we offered a seat at our table to a student with Down syndrome. We opened our doors to this gift from God, a beautiful little girl who just happened to have been born with an extra chromosome, into our kindergarten class. Her parents, Chris and Mary Ann Bain recently noted that after having one door closed on them and then being accepted at Faith Hope, *"The weight of the world was lifted off our shoulders. Our daughter was not being marginalized. Not only was she was being welcomed, she was being celebrated."*

Inclusion works in many ways. Studies show that by having the opportunity to learn alongside typically developing peers, children with special needs can realize their full potential. Additionally, typically developing peers experience a curriculum like no other as they experience first-hand the qualities of compassion, patience, tolerance, empathy and acceptance of all God's children. In a world that is in desperate need of these qualities, why do we put these children away into special classrooms when we can spread their gifts so freely? As noted by Deidre's teacher, Mrs. Betty Ann Shanley, *"The level of compassion we have seen from ALL students is mind-blowing."* Our faculty and students give Deidre 110% and she gives us all 200% in return each day. As a mom of a classmate recently noted, *"Dee had changed our entire family for the better, not just our daughter, but each one of us."* Shouldn't this be what we want for our Catholic school communities? We have the ability to make students more equipped to fully function in the world around them, a world that is full of all abilities. I believe in the future that our students will be better participants in their high school communities, better college roommates, better employees, better spouses and better parents. They will be better positioned to make a difference in the world around them and better equipped to handle disability if it hits close to home.

During Deirdre's first year at Faith Hope, I truly saw God in the words and actions of members of our school community. I saw skeptical teachers and parents become believers. I saw tough students become gentle. Perhaps a most memorable experience will always be the first grade girl, running down the hall, backpack flailing behind her, to tell me that she had "the best news." She was going to have a new cousin and that cousin was going to be born with Down syndrome! This student knew the treasure, you could see the joy and excitement in her face. I smiled quietly, as I knew this precious little girl would lead the charge of acceptance in her extended family. Perhaps, at the tender age of six, she would be a life-line to a new mom, who may be grieving the child that she had hoped to deliver. Perhaps this little, toothless girl, would help her aunt realize the acceptance that her soon-to-be-born child would find waiting for him/her in this world.

And perhaps my best memories of inclusion will always be of a staff member, a teacher assistant named Francesca, also with the diagnosis of Down syndrome, who keeps the staff light-hearted on the toughest days, who connects with children that appear to be having a hard time, and who shows us all that there is great possibility in disability. This past January, Francesca was trained to be a Eucharistic Minister. At an all-school mass during Catholic Schools Week, I watched her distribute communion to her mother and grandmother, as well as the student body. There were tears of pride in the eyes of all who know and love her, but especially her junior high students who are better because of her presence. Francesca showed us that her disability does not define her. She is a teacher, colleague, and is now living and sharing her Catholic faith as a Eucharistic minister.

Most importantly, Catholic Social Teaching tells us that as Catholic schools, we are called to build the Kingdom of God, which includes all his children, regardless of their abilities, challenges, or physical condition. We are required to look at children with the eyes of Christ, and to love and accept the beauty of their differences. Catholic school inclusion answers the hope of Pope Benedict XVI that "no child should be denied his or her right to an education in faith, which in turn nurtures the soul of a nation."

Pope Francis said, "Each of us has a treasure inside." At Faith Hope, we have committed ourselves to opening our hearts and minds to the possibilities by looking past disabilities in order to find this treasure in each of God's children. In doing so, we are modelling patience, tolerance, compassion, empathy, acceptance and a desire to advocate for the marginalized. And like the seeds of a dandelion, these traits are spreading, creating a greater acceptance for all of God's children.

Article printed in NCEA Feb 2017. Published with permission. Katie Carden is a mom to 6 children, with her youngest son born with Down syndrome. She is an educator and Catholic School principal in Chicago who has a passion for Catholic School Inclusion.

Be The Change

Dr. Nigel Traylor

While it is unfortunate in our world today, all students (and many times us as adults) share in one way or another a common bond of being misrepresented, misjudged, and misunderstood. Whether a student is black, white, Hispanic, Asian, introvert or extrovert, straight or gay, rich or poor, a great learner or someone with a learning disability--we have all been that stranger in a strange land where we have been left feeling as if we don't have a place.

Why should any of these differences matter? Each one of us should be proud of who we are. We are meant to embrace our differences and should never have to apologize for them. Every student that comes through the doors of our schools should know that they are among a community that wants to make sure that they are respected, safe, loved, known, and served. I am so proud to say that at Bishop McNamara we never want any person to feel as though they have been alienated, defeated, deflated, or discouraged. This is a safe place where students come to learn, grow and be empowered leaders who are inspired by the gospel to go out and change the world. We strive to ensure all students, parents, faculty and staff know that we have all been fearfully and wonderfully made in the image of Christ.

Regardless of how we may see others behave in school, and out of school; regardless of the behavior of people who hold influential positions in our society, don't let those people alter your behavior. Make the conscious choice to Be The Change and be that positive light you want to see in this world! How do we do that? Start by being kind, support each other, and when you see someone struggling-reach out to help – that is the definition of inclusion.

Dr. Nigel A. Traylor serves as the Principal of Bishop McNamara High School in Forestville Maryland. He holds degrees from The University if Pennsylvania, Nova Southeastern University and the University of Georgia in Educational Leadership. He is dedicated to purposely helping all of his students to see God in all things and the face of Christ in all people, to transform themselves and society, to seek truth in all they do, and to be servant-leaders who seek to make the world a better place.

Actions Speak Louder Than Words

Cindy May

"Actions speak louder than words". It's a simple phrase, but one the Catholic Church and its leaders ought to consider when they remind followers about the value of all human life. It is astonishing that a community that is so strongly pro-life, that insists that its members respect and honor all human life, could abandon the families who follow these teachings. This abandonment occurs day after day all across America in Catholic schools that refuse to accept and educate children wit intellectual and developmental disabilities.

Surprised? I was. I am Catholic, and mother to five children – twins and triplets. From an early point in my triplet pregnancy, doctors suspected that one my triplets might have a genetic "enhancement" – specifically, Down syndrome. When I went to my priest for guidance and support, I admitted my fear of caring for a child with a disability, especially given that I would soon be the mother of five children, all under the age of 4. I wasn't sure I could handle the task. The priest looked confidently into my eyes and told me, "God will provide you and your family with the resources you need. You will see, your entire family will be blessed and benefit from this experience."

That priest was right. My daughter was one of the greatest blessings of my life, and after her birth I realized that she was, in most ways, just like her siblings. She learned to walk and talk and read and do all the other things kids do – albeit more slowly than her siblings – but successfully nonetheless. I was grateful for the faith the Church had cultivated in me during my 12 years in Catholic school, for without those teachings I might have made a very different decision about the pregnancy. Like most parents, I now find it difficult and even painful to fathom a life in which my daughter was never born, not simply because of the love I have for her, but because of the way she has transformed the lives of others.

Imagine my astonishment when I discovered that the very schools that instilled in me a belief that all human beings have worth were also the ones that refused to accept children with intellectual disabilities. When a parent of a child with special needs tries to enroll that child in Catholic school, they are all too often told, "We simply don't have the resources. We have so many other demands, and we have to educate our typical children." As a mother of twins and triplets, one of whom had Down syndrome, I understand competing demands, and I know what it feels like to be overwhelmed. I recognize that our school leaders and teachers may feel terrified, under-staffed, ill-prepared. But Catholic schools need to be given the same message that was given to me when I questioned my own ability to handle this task: All children have value. All children bring an essential element to the educational community. You will find the resources you need, and your school will benefit from this experience.

In discussing the benefits of inclusion, it is important to understand that long-term research shows that schools thrive when they include children with disabilities. As you might expect, there is an enormous benefit of inclusion for the children with disabilities. They are in an environment in which they are accepted and embraced, with appropriate role models and social interactions; as a result, their mathematical, linguistic and social skills are years ahead of those of children with disabilities who are segregated into separate, "special" classrooms.

Perhaps the surprising news is that typically-developing children also benefit greatly from inclusion. Numerous studies have documented that, contrary to popular belief, typically-developing students excel in inclusive classrooms. The test scores of non-disabled students in inclusive schools are as high (or higher) than those of students in non-inclusive schools, and measures of tolerance and comfort with diverse peoples are stronger. These data come largely from public schools, but there are indeed some Catholic schools around the country that have successfully implemented inclusive programs, and they have experienced these same successes. I have assisted with the inclusive process in some of these Catholic schools, and have witnessed the positive transformation first hand.

How is this so? Many falsely assume that when students with disabilities are included in classes with non-disabled students, they will consume more of the resources, attention, and time – and consequently students without disabilities will suffer. The data do not bear out this fear. Instead, teachers who include with students with disabilities in their classes learn new approaches and alternative styles, and these new techniques benefit all students. In addition, the culture of inclusion creates a learning environment in which all students have a sense of belonging. No student is marginalized, regardless of appearance or ability. Those are the environments in which learning blossoms.

Beyond the academic advantages of inclusion, the Catholic Church must recognize the social and moral benefits of including children with disabilities in their classrooms. By living and learning with children who have disabilities, our typically developing children learn about empathy, reciprocity, patience and understanding. They learn the genuine value of people who are different. They learn that having a disability does not equate with being unable or less than. They learn all these things by living them every day. What better lessons can we convey to our future business leaders, doctors, teachers, policy makers, and parents? These lessons will help students recognize that disability is just another form of diversity, that people with disabilities are an important part of the everyday world, and that people with disabilities deserve full and authentic participation in all parts of society. When they encounter disability as adults they will respond with optimism, respect, and opportunity rather than fear, ignorance, and intolerance.

When Catholic schools reject students with disabilities – even to provide them with "separate but equal" Catholic education – they send a very powerful message to the entire community. The message is this: Yes, parents, you should find value in every life. Yes, families, you should love and nurture and embrace those who are different, those with special needs. But........NO, we will not be there to support or educate those children. They do not belong in our schools with our children without disabilities.

Despite our message of acceptance and support for all life, we cannot find a way to include students with intellectual disabilities in our regular schools.

The time has come for the Catholic Church to teach in life what it preaches in word. The Catholic Church has historically been the champion of the underprivileged and the underserved. It has embraced the poor, the sick, the sinners – even the criminals.

The Church provides social, health, and educational programs for unwed mothers, for the poor in foreign countries, for dying patients, for convicted felons. But a Catholic Church that is truly pro-life and not simply pro-birth will also advocate for and support people with disabilities throughout their lives, and will start by opening the doors of its schools to all students. An essential component of promoting life is the development of authentic opportunity and hope for individuals who have historically been rejected, and taking a pro-life stance without accepting students with disabilities in our schools is astonishingly hypocritical and undermines every effort to recognize the value in all human life.""

Cindi May, PhD is a cognitive scientist and mother of six children, two of whom have Down syndrome. Her work focuses on research and advocacy for people with disabilities.

All Are Welcome Here

Sheila Klich

Traveling down Western Avenue, on the north side of Chicago, the red brick façade of St. Matthias School looks like any other school in the neighborhood. Little would one suspect that there is a revolution going on inside, and St. Matthias is the right place for a revolution! Its diversity and strong community make it an environment like no other. The real excitement, though, is around inclusion.

Historically, many Catholic schools have not always served those with special needs. For me, as an educator, this attitude always felt unfair to the students, family and school community. It went against the Gospel values of love and acceptance and always rubbed me the wrong way.

As a teacher, through professional development offered by Loyola University, an action research project done for the University of Notre Dame and the mentoring of like-minded administration, I was given the freedom to challenge that line of thought. I broadened my approach to include differentiated instruction in my classes and a small pull-out group for additional support. As Principal, through participating in the All Are Welcome Program offered by Loyola University, I now have the skills and confidence to expand the vision of an inclusive Catholic school. The entire school community is working towards a vision of inclusion where students and teachers are supported. Intentional planning around welcoming diverse learners remains a key piece of the school's mission.

I have creatively hired with this mission in mind, an Inclusive Learning Coordinator, who is now a crucial member of the administrative team. She helps to streamline services, coordinate resources and deliver professional development. Her creativity and energetic approach toward guiding the teachers, students and families helps create the welcoming, positive energy teachers need to try new things and approach serving all their students.

Differentiation in the classroom is now the name of the game. Teachers scaffold their instruction and the materials used, so that all learners can access information. Students receive support around how they complete assignments, such as written essays. Teachers explore multi-modal avenues for presenting and assessing information. Brain breaks and movement are a regular part of the day for some students.

As with many Catholic schools and good revolutions, finances and budgetary constraints abound. Creativity, resourcefulness and a refusal to surrender have allowed us to leverage a number of resources. The Archdiocese of Chicago, Loyola University, Aspire Illinois, and even a few nearby Chicago Public Schools, LEEP Forward and other organizations have worked with teachers, students and families to provide resources to strengthen our programs.

The National Catholic Educational Association stands out as another strong inclusion supporter.

The St. Matthias School community is excited about the attention the NCEA is giving inclusion. Catholic schools serious about their own inclusion revolutions really should consider attending. A good revolution requires strong allies!

Are we there yet? Has our revolution come to a successful conclusion? No.

We continue to need funding for programs and resources, more avenues for professional development on differentiation. We need to broaden MTSS in our school so that it guides us in our work with all our students.

There are students we cannot serve as successfully as we'd like. However, their needs and their voices push us forward in our quest to "widen our center" and be a community for an even more diverse population.

There's just one other thing worth noting, should you find yourself on Western Avenue in Chicago; it's our sign, which reads "All are welcome here". It's our calling, our mantra, and our challenge for the future.

Sheila Klich is a Catholic school principal in the archdiocese of Chicago. She believes Catholic schools are an important part of the inclusion movement. Article printed in NCEA 2017. Published with permission

"If we are to have Catholic schools,
what children are most in need of
our special love and care?

Shouldn't it be those who,
according to Catholic social teaching,
might be considered
'the least among us' and
'those to which the Kingdom
of heaven belongs' ?"
(Matthew 19:11)

Dr. Mary Carlson, from Marquette University, in Milwaukee, Wisconsin's
Ph.D. Dissertation entitled: *Special Education as a Moral Mandate for Catholic Schools.*

"for I am fearfully
and wonderfully
made: marvelous
are thy works"

Psalm 139:14

Fear: Who's in Control?

Francesca Pellegrino

Fear, not to mention anger, can move us into action or be paralyzing. I learned this all too well from personal experience, the kind, quite honestly, I would have preferred to avoid.

My life path and purpose changed when my son was born with a disability twenty-five years ago. Had someone told me before he came along that so many years later I would be advocating for children with disabilities in Catholic schools, I would have dismissed the idea as idle folly! However, we often do not know or understand God's plan for us. My son's early years were fraught with medical issues, with him in and out of intensive care. I became angry and dejected and ultimately suffered a crisis of faith. Thanks to the support of some key people in my life, a transformation began to take place. Something within me had stirred. Thus began an amazing faith journey that would take me from hopelessness, to action, to the creation of the Catholic Coalition for Special Education (CCSE).

My mother taught me all about strength, tenacity, and courage and how to stand up for my own rights and for those of Alex, who cannot advocate for himself. Moreover, my experience with Alex taught me to appreciate many things I otherwise would not, such as trains! Then there are those things I wish I had not had to learn at all, such as all that medical terminology when Alex was in hospital.

The challenges have been many, but ultimately they have given me strength and character enough to heed the call to reach out to those who need help, support, love, understanding, and peace. The Lord presents us with these challenges because He knows this is how to help us grow and make us stronger both as individuals and as a society.

Years ago when Alex was very young, doctors recommended a certain, obscure operation they said was essential "or your child could die". My reaction, borne of fear of losing my son, was of course, "let's schedule it," while my husband's more logical reasoning led us to question whether it was the right procedure for him. We then realized that we didn't like what Alex's life might look like after the operation. Ultimately, he did not have the operation and he is doing just fine! As a couple, it was probably one of the best and most significant decisions we ever made together.

Then when he was a bit older, like all other boys his age, he loved to run and climb everything he could find. One day at a birthday party, he climbed onto monkey bars that were very high off the ground and I couldn't reach him. Out of fear, I would have told him to get down immediately to avoid getting hurt, but he was having so much fun, I couldn't let my fears hold him back, so I stood underneath him knowing that we'd both get hurt if he actually fell. He made it across just fine and I learned a very important parenting lesson. Give him the space and confidence he needs to grow and develop.

Fast forward to age eighteen. Alex has completed twelfth grade and is now in his transition program. One of the key elements of the program is travel training. And, no surprise, fear creeps in again. My loved one is going to start using city buses and metro trains in the capital of the U.S.A. Yikes! Alarm bells start resounding in my head, and visions of him being hit by a car as he tries to cross a busy main street begin to occupy my imagination. But, Alex's transition teacher knows him sufficiently well to know what he is capable of accomplishing. Equally important, that transition teacher also has confidence in his own abilities as a teacher. Thanks to all the available technology, I can keep an eye on my son, from a distance, without hovering and at the same time allow him to grow into a young man who can now take public transportation to his two paid jobs. The ability to use public transportation gives him so many opportunities that would otherwise be out of reach. Like everyone else in our community who commutes to work via public transportation, he sees people he knows along the way and he enjoys this aspect of his commute. This does not mean I don't worry about him out and about in the community. However, recently when the train broke down and he had to take a special shuttle bus to a stop he doesn't typically use, I tried to intervene, but he firmly assured me he had his alternate itinerary all planned out in his head. An hour and a half later than usual, he arrived home safe and sound. Amazingly, he always seems to rise to the challenge. Thank you, Lord! I continue to marvel at the transformative impact that Alex has had on my life.

Just as Catholic parents are led on unexpected journeys when they are graced with a child with a disability, educators and administrators are similarly led when they heed the call to include children with disabilities in their classrooms. Often educators and administrators report that including children with disabilities provides countless, unexpected blessings to their entire school community even though initially they might have had some trepidation about doing so. One school principal reported that upon retirement she will look back on her experiences of including children with disabilities as some of the fondest and proudest moments of her teaching career.[1]

Each child is an unrepeatable gift from God. Each one has his or her special gifts to share, and we must never take this most precious gift for granted. Children represent our dreams, our hopes, and our future. Life would be meaningless without them. Let's give our children with disabilities the same chances and opportunities we want for all our children and not let our own fears hold them back or hinder us.

Francesca Pellegrino is a leader in inclusive education for Catholic schools, is married with one son, who inspired her to create Catholic Coalition for Special Education. This calling makes her a passionate advocate for children and youth with disabilities.

[1]Francesca Pellegrino, excerpt from the Forward to *Including Students with Development Disabilities in Catholic Schools – Guiding Principles for Administrators and Teachers*, published by the Catholic Coalition for Special Education.

Maybelle at Nativity

Cindy May

In this moment in time when we hear so much negativity, so much frustration, so much disgust about the world, I want to take this opportunity to share some pure, unadulterated gratitude. I am grateful for Nativity School in Charleston, SC.

To understand my gratitude, it might help if you know a little bit about me.

Like many Catholic moms, I have lots of children. Eighteen years ago, God blessed me with twins, and three years later he blessed me with triplets. So, we had our hands full.

Like many people raised in the Catholic tradition, I was eager to send my children to Catholic school so that they might receive the same strong education and moral grounding that I had received in my twelve years of Catholic schooling. There was just one hiccup: one of my triplets, Grace, was born with Down syndrome. You might be surprised to learn that fifteen years ago when Grace was born, children with Down syndrome were not welcome at many—in fact most—of the Catholic schools in Charleston.

I was surprised. It was in Catholic school that I learned that every human has value, that we all have talents, that we are all perfect in God's eyes, and that if we trust in God, he will give us the resources we need to face all challenges. How could the very schools where I had learned these lessons turn away children simply because of their genetic makeup?

I promised myself that I would work with our schools so that Grace could have the chance to learn alongside her siblings and her peers, and so that our Catholic schools could understand the value that Grace and other children like her bring to our communities.

I did not get that chance. Not with Grace. When Grace was three years old, she was diagnosed with leukemia. She lived only six weeks longer. My precious child who had changed my world, and who I was confident would change the world for others, was gone.

To be honest, I wanted to crawl under a rock and stay there forever. But although Grace was gone, the needs of children with Down syndrome and other disabilities were not. My friends and colleagues and fellow advocates were still searching for schools that would embrace and educate their kids.

One such friend, Alison, was a fellow teacher at the College of Charleston. Alison had a little girl with Down syndrome named Maybelle, and Alison wanted Maybelle to learn to read and write, to follow instructions, to make friends, to do her best, to be part of her community.

So Alison and I searched together for a place that would include Maybelle. As you can imagine, I turned to the Catholic schools. In fact, I started at the very same school where I sent my own typically-developing children. I was confident that Maybelle would be welcomed at this school, which prided itself on embracing diversity and nurturing the gifts of each child. In fact, I had chosen the school because it espoused all the values and teachings that underlie inclusion. And they had an offer of mentorship from Bishop England High School right down the road, a Catholic high school that had successfully included students with intellectual disabilities for more than a decade. But I was wrong. Maybelle was not welcome. Her type of diversity was not embraced, nor were they willing to nurture her gifts. They did not even try; they simply said NO. I was heartbroken and quite honestly my faith was shaken.

But then I remembered that Patti Dukes was the principal at Nativity School on James Island. I knew Patti because our children had all swum on the same city team years earlier, but I was less familiar with Nativity because it was far from where I lived. I nervously called Patti to see if she might consider accepting Maybelle. I will never forget Patti's words on the phone - before she had even met Maybelle: "I'm not positive we will meet all of Maybelle's needs, but

YES, let's try. Of course she is welcome and we'll do the best we can."

Let's try. That is all God asks of us: to try.

In trying, Patti and the entire community at Nativity have changed the world for Maybelle and also for all the students at Nativity.

Maybelle is now in third grade. She masters fifteen spelling words and eight new vocabulary words each week. Her handwriting is terrible, but she is allowed to type her answers. She can add and subtract three-digit numbers and is learning to multiply. Like many of her classmates, she does not love homework. She does love PE and library. Last year, she made her First Reconciliation and First Holy Communion with her class. For the past two years, she has played basketball on the school team. Last weekend she made her very first basket in an official game.

Because of Nativity, Maybelle has a community. She is learning. She has friends. She has a very promising future.

Because of Maybelle, students at Nativity are learning lessons that are impossible to teach from a textbook. They know - beyond a shadow of a doubt - that all people are valued. They see that people who seem very different may in fact be very much alike. They understand that some people have to work harder than others to learn, and perhaps that encourages them to work a little harder, too.

Most importantly, they are learning that life throws you unexpected curve balls, but God and your community are there for you.

Maybelle was thrown a huge curve ball last year. Maybelle lost her mom. My friend Alison was diagnosed with a brain tumor and passed away just before Maybelle's eighth birthday.

When Alison died, Maybelle joined our family and together we had to adjust in many ways. Through it all, the one constant source of support, the one place that we knew Maybelle was welcome and would be valued and challenged, was Nativity. Like us, they sometimes struggle to meet all of Maybelle's needs. But they are fabulous communicators and they team with others (thank you Bishop England! thank you Maybelle's therapists!) when needed to find a way.

Most of us face unexpected curve balls in life. To handle those curve balls, we need, above all else, the knowledge that God and our community are with us. I am so grateful that Maybelle lives with that knowledge. Because of Nativity, she has a community. Because of Nativity, she can feel God's love with her every day. And now that Maybelle has joined our family, we, too, live with the blessing of the Nativity family. I am so grateful for the leadership, the teachers, the families, and the students at Nativity, where they have taken what others consider to be extraordinary or even impossible and turned it into their every ordinary. They tried. They succeeded. We are all blessed.

Cindi May is a mom to six children, including two girls with Down syndrome. She and her family live in South Carolina, where they are blessed with many inclusive opportunities.

Journey Of Mazes

LeeAnn Armitage

"Cowardice asks the question, is it safe? Expediency asks the question, is it polite? Vanity asks the question, is it popular? But conscience asks the question, is it right? And there comes a time when one must take a position that is neither safe, nor polite, nor popular - but one must take it because it's right."

Martin Luther King, Jr spoke those words in the 1950's as he was advocating for African-American civil rights in America. He was all about using non-violent ways to show your civil disobedience. Many of his messages were tied to his faith as a Baptist minister. He understood the connection between having a faith to lean on and questioning authority when the fight was a noble one which, when fought graciously and with conviction, would ultimately lead to the glory of God and not personal gain or personal agendas. I think that's how he knew which fights to fight, and which to abandon - by asking would the outcome give glory to God?

In 2013, my husband and I started the conversation with our Catholic parish school to include our son, Christopher in their school. Chris has Down syndrome. Children with Down syndrome are not typically included in catholic schools. And it certainly had never been done at Mary, Queen of Peace. It was a bold question we were asking, yet our story is not unique or special. Many catholic families around the country have approached their parish schools asking for their children with disabilities to be included in the school with their siblings and friends. Many have knocked and been turned away. No room at the Inn.

We heard all of the "reasons" every other family has heard. Teachers aren't qualified. We have no money to hire and train teachers. What happens when the academic gap gets too large between the child and his peers? What will it look like in 7th grade science when the child cannot read yet? The community will not support this. We have no money. The public schools have what he needs, you can send him there. This is an academic institution, therefore the child must make significant academic gains. Won't this bring down our school's test scores? The child will be disruptive. Your child's needs will take away from the other kids in the class. Did I mention: We have no money?

We heard them all. We methodically took all of the "reasons" and attempted to address or solve each of them. Each time we were just met with another "reason" and it made us ask what is the REAL reason Catholic schools choose not to practice inclusion of children with intellectual disabilities? Many families have been deeply hurt by the rejection. Some have even left the catholic faith altogether because of this issue.

My husband and I chose to keep advocating. There were many ups and downs in the two year process. MQP allowed Chris to attend preschool for one year. After what we considered a successful year for him, we were told he was could not come back for kindergarten. We fought the decision. They fought back. We fought more. They fought even more. The first day of kindergarten came and went and my son was not in class. We went "underground" and stayed quiet for several months licking our wounds, weary after all the fighting. The crazy thing was, our parish community got it. They were supportive of the school accepting Chris. But fear of the unknown is a powerful thing.

This whole time I kept hearing the whisper of God's voice to keep going. God was telling me very clearly that all of the 'No' voices I was hearing were the devil's work. God told me to keep going. I imagined myself in one of those hedge or corn mazes.

You take a turn and run into a wall, so you turn around and go another way, and you keep bumping into dead ends or maybe you gain some ground. When you're in the maze you can't see the way out but if someone was looking down on the maze, they could see that with just one more turn, you would be out and free. I thought of God looking down on us and this journey and I kept hearing Him say, "Keep going. You're almost there. Just keep going!" The "No's" were still louder than the whisper of God.

We chose to lean on and focus on that whisper rather than the loud and overpowering No's.

We decided to home school Chris for kindergarten. We did not believe that the public school option was right for him – we had visited our public schools and knew he would just be segregated. Around Thanksgiving, my husband heard the battle cry once more and was moved to start asking yet again. He knew many had fought as hard as we had. He knew that in order to be successful we needed to have a sustained effort and we needed to work through people in our parish. We also realized it wasn't just about us or Chris, but about all the children and families that had struggled and the families yet to come. We had a systemic problem and we had to look beyond our own children and sustain the effort not to be personally successful, but to sacrifice and gradually change the system. There were a lot of passionate people on our side. We needed to keep fighting this God-given task. We very much believe we were directly called to fight for this in our own parish.

Not believing we would be successful with Christopher we started a not-for-profit foundation "One Classroom" (www.oneclassroom.com) to raise money so that grants could be given to schools in St. Louis who would welcome children with special needs, if not our school and son, maybe some other school and family. The One Classroom Foundation was modeled after the F.I.R.E. Foundation in KC. They have been incredible mentors to us along the way.

By the efforts of our fellow parishioners we were able to organize a bus trip the following Spring to the Kansas City diocese to see inclusion in catholic schools in action. One Classroom Foundation sponsored the trip and invited many parish and school stakeholders to take the trip with us including our own pastor and principal. And it was transforming for everyone. Only the Holy Spirit can change hearts the way they were changed that day. Seeing inclusion in action, in a Catholic school context, and witnessing the impact on both children with special needs and the typically developing children was extraordinarily impactful.

Since the day we returned, it has been like a boulder rolling down the hill and we couldn't get a program started fast enough! I spent the week after we returned laughing with each new development! Laughing at the incredibleness that was happening all around me. It was unbelievable and I think I was laughing because it was all so improbable. Only God can create something like this!

And so on August 19, 2015 my son was in full uniform and lined up with his peers from preschool ready to start their first day of First Grade at Mary, Queen of Peace School. The really beautiful thing is that One Classroom was able to support two other children with Down syndrome starting in kindergarten on that same first day! Yes, the Holy Spirit has sent three children with Down syndrome to our parish. This journey has been divinely guided since the beginning and we were always on God's time, not ours.

We trusted that this fight was about more than Christopher. The realization of this dream brings glory to God in every way and to many. Jesus would not turn our children away. We are called to be the hands and eyes and heart of Jesus here on earth.

How we treat the least of our brothers and sisters is how we would treat Jesus himself. We fought this fight for Christopher and others like him, but we fought the fight because it was the right thing to do.

We tried to always make decisions based on taking the high road and not going rogue and demanding this for our son or bullying the school to accept him. It wasn't always the easy thing to do and I have spent more time than I'm willing to admit, on my knees in the confessional trying to reconcile my feelings. I think that has paid off in the end and gained us the respect of the administration we were once fighting.

We are now (in 2018) working in complete cooperation on the inclusion program and today support five children with significant special needs at Mary Queen of Peace. I have a new respect for our administration - changing your decision is never easy - but I respect that they were able to take in new information and then make new decisions and most of all I respect their leap of faith. Fear of the unknown is a powerful thing, but faith in God is more powerful!

As of February 2018, One Classroom has support of our Archbishop and Catholic Education office. We have helped five schools in total welcome children with significant special needs and are working with families at another six schools! God has shown us that we can do so much more with his help. But He has also shown us that you have to keep pushing while you're praying!!

I truly offer up to God all of the suffering this journey has asked me to endure.

Someday, perhaps, our catholic schools will more readily accept children with intellectual disabilities because of our fight and can stand on our shoulders just as we are standing on other's shoulders now. In the kingdom of God, we are all in One Classroom.

LeeAnn Armitage and her husband Tony live in Webster Groves, MO with their children, Mary and Christopher. They believe all children deserve to be in their Catholic school communities. Tony & LeeAnn are founders of One Classroom, a non-profit dedicated to supporting the inclusion of children with special needs in the Catholic schools of the Archdiocese of St. Louis." (www. one-classroom.com)

Inclusion Begins in the Heart

Anne Maddock

"Inclusion begins in our hearts. It begins with affirmation. We should open our hearts to one another and recognize the strengths of every person... When we open our hearts and our community to the gifts each person brings, we are all strengthened."

—*Cardinal Bernardin*

Fortunately for my family, there are individuals who took his words and turned them into reality. Twenty two years ago, when our fourth child was born with Down syndrome, my family was concerned that Francesca would not receive the Catholic education her siblings were getting. Due to some wonderful angels in our lives, Sr. Mary Lou Wetzell at Queen of All Saints and Sr. Barbara Jean Ciszek at Cardinal Bernardin Early Childhood Center, Francesca was fully included in Catholic schools from age 4-11. Francesca thrived in this setting. CBECC is a Catholic Montessori that includes 3 children with special needs per classroom. This was a perfect setting for Francesca. Her self confidence soared as she was even given the opportunity to mentor younger students.

When Francesca aged out of CBECC, we felt a move to the suburbs was the best option to continue her education. Our older children were able to continue at a Catholic high school and Francesca would have access to excellent public schools. Although it was only a 10 mile move, the change in neighborhood was difficult for Francesca. When she said, "I'm really going to miss God when we move" it brought me to tears.

Francesca had a wonderful inclusive education in the public schools. She made lifelong friends and had excellent teachers. For our family though, there was always missing pieces for Francesca: no daily prayers, no uniforms, and no school masses for her.

Fast forward to Francesca completing school. Through an internship at Francesca's high school transition program, we met another angel, Katie Carden. She is the principal of Faith, Hope and Charity School. After interning with a job coach for one year, Katie offered Francesca a job. This was a dream come true for all of us! Francesca has loved every minute of the past two years as a teacher's aide. Working in a Catholic school is more than a job. It is being part of a loving, caring community. FHC has welcomed Francesca with open arms. She is truly part of a wonderful team.

She attends teacher retreats, was included in the teacher Secret Santa and even enjoys an beer with her colleagues at the staff Christmas party! She works as an aide in art, music and second grade reading. Francesca was beaming when she went back to school after her two week Christmas break. She literally laughed out loud when she got out of the car. How many teachers can say they are that enthusiastic to get back to work after break?

"The sky's the limit" has been the attitude of the staff at FHC. It is a beautiful, nurturing environment. There are countless benefits to being in a Catholic school. Francesca helps with the choir on the altar at mass every Wednesday. As a newly minted Eucharistic Minister, she distributes communion as well.

The Chicago Catholic school community has been a blessing for Francesca and our family. The support and love she has received have given her the opportunity to reach her potential. How proud Cardinal Bernardin would be if he could see how far the Chicago Catholic schools have come.

Anne Maddock is a mom to 4 children, the youngest of whom has Down syndrome. As a Catholic family they hope/dream/pray for inclusion in catholic schools to become the new norm

Catholic Inclusion for Our Michael

Susan Schuller

We are strong supporters of Catholic education, and our first four children were all attending Greenwich Catholic School when Michael was born with Down syndrome in 2006.

Once it was time to start school, we were told that the services Michael needed were only at the public school. Our hearts sank. I considered for a moment switching all of our children over to the public schools, but my husband, Dan, would not even consider it. Thank goodness! As we got to know Michael, we realized what a great learner he was. Sure, most things took him longer and required more repetition, but he was a truly eager learner!

Our Catholic schools, first in Connecticut and now in Pennsylvania, embraced Michael. In fact, when we were moving, our principal from Connecticut, Patrice Kopas, even secretly mailed to our new principal in Pennsylvania, Bud Tosti, the Down syndrome wristband that she wore daily. Imagine my surprise when in a meeting at the new school, the wristband caught my eye. Mr. Tosti confirmed that Mrs. Kopas had "passed the torch" in sending it to him. Now, he wears it daily!

The schools didn't just allow or accept Michael, they appreciate him and treat him with dignity and respect. They modify the curriculum so that he learns alongside his friends. The academic integrity is maintained, as he is exposed to the same curriculum, but he is responsible for mastering less of it.

Michael talks about his friends constantly. His list of friends is close to 100! He plays basketball on our St. Monica Parish fourth grade team, and serves at 7:30am Mass with support from another peer. Two weeks ago, when we hosted a concert on inclusion, Life Makes a Difference, over two dozen school friends chose to participate with him.

Our biggest fear when we received Michael's diagnosis at his birth was that he would be treated badly by others and would never be loved outside of our family. We felt that we would need to protect him from the world outside. Instead, our Greenwich Catholic community was so supportive of us and brought us six weeks' worth of meals between Michael's birth and his open-heart surgery at three months. We were so grateful for the love and support. We saw the beauty of what inclusion did within our own family and really wanted the same for the other children that we loved so deeply at our Catholic school. I realized quickly that children are very comfortable with inclusion if their concerns and questions are addressed. It really is the adults that have the biggest fears of inclusion. Many of us didn't grow up with it and we let fear get in the way. Our children should grow up knowing and appreciating those with disabilities so that as adults they will consider employing them.

I feel so strongly that the Catholic educational system needs to make inclusion a priority and choose to train and plan for inclusion. Meaningful inclusion brings hope.

It truly is pro-life to include all.

I know that if I had seen inclusion before Michael was born, I would have had a much different perspective at his birth. One person can make a difference. Dan and I never dreamed that Michael could attend a Catholic school with his siblings, until it happened.

We are so grateful and want others to have the same opportunity.

Susan Schuller is the mom of six children, the fifth of whom has DS. So grateful for all of the champions in our lives who support us and meaningful inclusion.

Including JoJo

Michele McGown

My son attends an amazing private Catholic school in Carlsbad. The principle at his school reached out and requested a meeting with me. Naturally, I thought, "Uh-ohhhhhh! What did my son do?" Ha! But, it turns out it had nothing to do with him at all.

It was about my daughter JoJo.

She is our youngest, and she happens to ROCK the extra Down syndrome chromosome.

The principal wanted to discuss JoJo. She wanted to have JoJo attend their school. See, my daughter and son don't go to school together. My daughter goes to public school. The principal asked to go over went her IEP, programs, and therapies. We talked about learning methods, how she learns best, and what modifications are needed. The principal wanted so badly to put into place a program to include JoJo into their school. They currently have several children in attendance with mild IEP issues, but she wanted to learn and create a game plan to practice full inclusion. Nothing scared her, she was ready to move forward. The biggest hurdle? Money.

Unfortunately, my husband and I were not prepared financially to take on the burden of the tuition plus pay for the salary of an aide as well. We continue to hope things will change. Paying for an aide is too big of a burden for us to take on, as I know it is for many families. It is heartbreaking for us that our children don't attend school together. We would love for JoJo to have a Catholic education. She deserves it. But, it cannot be a burden to our family and it shouldn't be to other families either. We pray that this situation will change. We pray that someday our two children can attend Catholic school together. In the meantime, JoJo does attend the school parish's Religious Education program, which is a part of the church community. And as a family, we are active in our church and attend mass regularly, and everyone knows and loves JoJo. I pray daily for two things:

1. that people will see the beauty in JoJo and see how perfect she truly is

2. that a Catholic education is affordable for each child and family that desire a Catholic education.

"Give generously your contribution so that the Catholic school never becomes a fall-back option or a meaningless alternative among the various educational institutions. Collaborate so that Catholic education has the face of new humanism. ... Strive to make Catholic schools truly open to all." –Pope Francis.

Michele McGown is a devout Catholic. She is also wife and mother to two kids, a twelve-year-old son and an eight-year-old daughter, who has Down syndrome. It's been an incredibly positive journey.

John Paul's Essay

John Paul Lavallee

I have many friends with autism, Down syndrome and other disabilities. Some of them would have been aborted if their parents did not respect their lives. If this happened, there would be fewer people on the planet. Many people say this is good, because large populations are too hard on the earth's resources, but I believe that the earth can sustain every person God creates. People with autism would not get a chance to write a book about their experience, or be a genius, or be a good friend if they were aborted.

Many people with Down syndrome, 9 out of 10, are aborted every year because of a genetic test that can predict this condition before birth. This is sad and evil because these babies cannot defend themselves. All of us are being deprived of a chance to love and serve most children with Down syndrome, and to receive the love and kindness they grow up to give. This is a big problem because we live in a rich, powerful, and smart society, but this society is not generous or welcoming to any kind of life that seems weak, but is actually just different. I do not think this is smart at all. In fact, this injustice makes me angry at the people who encourage it. It shows that some people think they know better than God who are the perfect people to create.

I worry that something like this persecution could happen to people with autism if a similar genetic test is developed to predict autism. As a 14 year-old boy with autism, I know from personal experience that there are many things I can do without help. I love the world, and especially people. I love learning about the world, and spending time with my friends at Our Lady of Lourdes School. At my school, I am accepted along with everybody else. Some of us have disabilities, and some do not. None of us pretend we are perfect. I am glad to have a voice to say what I think about respecting every life. I know my voice is needed just as much as the voices of all my friends.

I like learning about new discoveries that scientists are making about autism. I hope these discoveries will help me, and many other people, some day. But, if these discoveries are used to kill us before birth instead of helping us grow up to share our special gifts, then I will be very sad. I will wonder what is good about science after all. It is important to talk about this problem now because we want to help people with Down syndrome to be loved and given life, just as much as we want this for people with every disability and for people with no disabilities. To respect life means knowing that God creates life, and remembering that everyone God creates is very good. Respecting life is another way to love God. Who can live without that?

John Paul Lavallee is a rising senior at Bishop McNamara High School in Maryland. He is grateful for inclusive Catholic education. His favorite subject is government and politics.

Dear 8th Graders

Beth Foraker

Way back in the fall of 2005, you entered kindergarten and a little experiment was going on.

You had a student in your class with an extra chromosome, otherwise known as Down syndrome.

No one came out and told you about this student and you just accepted him the way you accepted all of the other children in your class.

He couldn't run as fast as you could.

He couldn't write as well as you could.

He couldn't speak clearly.

And yet, he was part of you.

You figured it out.

You naturally, without any adult intervention, knew that this guy needed some support.

You let him use a different kind of basket when you played two on two basketball.

You threw the ball a bit differently so that he could catch it more often.

You walked a little slower to be by his side.

You accepted him.

Did you know you had a choice?

Not really...because we tricked you.

We just put him in your kindergarten class --

where kindergarteners just want to have fun.

*****

When Patrick was born, as soon as he was born, the doctor whisked him away, checked him all over and brought him back to

196

us a few hours later with a new label:

Down syndrome.

The doctor closed the door.

He put a sign on the door telling others not to visit us.

He didn't even let Jack or Mary Kate come in to see their little brother.

He thought this label would take some getting used to.

He thought we would be crying and scared.

He wanted us to have time.

He was coming from a good place...trying to be kind...but in truth, he was being cruel.

You know why??

He never went to school alongside someone who had this label.

He was afraid of it.

He didn't understand it.

He thought it was worth grieving.

Patrick did not get a celebration in those first hours of his birth.

No joy.

No laughing and photo-ops.

A whole lot of serious.

Can you imagine?

Probably the one person who is as joy-filled as could be and that was his welcome.

Maybe that's why he celebrates birthdays, all birthdays, in the biggest way possible now.

What was it like when you were born?

Oh, how your family celebrated!

How loved and awaited you were.

*****

So here we are nine years after beginning the experiment.

1,520 days you've been together.

Only 100 left until graduation.

I can't thank you enough for your acceptance.

Your grace.

Your friendship and kindness...

you know why?

Because you weren't nice out of pity or because morally you thought you should or because you were trying to be nice or even

because your parents told you to be nice.

You were accepting because you had the chance to get to know someone before you knew his label.

Best of all, Patrick had this chance.

That was our dearest hope for Patrick...

at St. James he could be Jack and Mary Kate's little brother.

He didn't have to be "Patrick with Down syndrome".

He got to just be Patrick.

If only you could know how profound that gift is.

Everywhere else, and I mean everywhere else, he is "Patrick with Down syndrome".

Here, in this little school of 300, he is label-less.

It's grace in the ordinary.every.single.day.

Did you know that Patrick will be the first person with Down syndrome to graduate from a Catholic school in our entire diocese???

He's the only person I know that has Down syndrome and is on student council, anywhere.

Do you know that because of your acceptance and the way your class has shown the school and the bigger world how to be as

people that you are changing the world?

For the better.

Do you know that still to this day principals and priests at other schools say no when a family that has a child with Down

Syndrome asks to go to their parish school??

That craziness still happens.

Why?

Because that principal or that priest didn't go to school alongside of people with disabilities.

They're scared and ignorant.

They don't realize just how normal it is

Someday you might be a principal.

Or a teacher.

Or a banker.

Or a parent.

I know that your kindness and awareness will be reflected in those jobs.

I can't wait to see what you do with your level of justice and equality and care.

I'm so excited about our future.

Because of you.

(And your parents, of course.)

Let's make the last 100 days the best yet.

Now you know the experiment.

You can tell your side of the story.

Share what you know.

Share your experiences.

Share with the world what equality and social justice looks like and feels like...

wait, it just feels normal....

like how it's supposed to be.

Exactly, my friends.

Never tolerate segregation or separation.

Anywhere.

You know the truth.

Together, we're better.

Beth Foraker-Mom to four kids - her third child, Patrick, has Down Syndrome. She works with beginning teachers at UC Davis and is the founder and director of The National Catholic Board on Full Inclusion

Ave Is Our Little Miracle

Lyn Cassidy

Ave was born with Down syndrome, two holes in her heart, a hearing deficit, and eye issues. During the first several months we just focused on getting her to eat well and gain weight. She was so very little. Some of the issues she had we didn't know a thing about. We had an appointment and testing with the pediatric cardiologist, and he confirmed there were two holes in her heart, although she had no symptoms. We had tentatively planned to go Rome with friends and family for the canonization of Blessed Pope John Paul II and Blessed Pope John XXIII (now Saint John Paul II and Saint John XXIII). Now the trip was on hold!

Gratefully within a week or two, the doctor cleared us to travel. We set our next appointment with the cardiologist for May 23, one month after our return from Rome. At that time, she would have another exam and echocardiogram to see if there was any progress in the closing of the two holes in her heart.

So, off we went! Ave was just three months old, and we were graced with an amazing Easter trip to Italy.

We had planned ahead. We had requested free tickets through the Pontifical College of North America in Rome for a Papal Audience in St. Peter's Square. We received our instructions of where to go and to sit in our designated spot. The Pope would drive through the Square and hopefully we would get to see him. We got up at 5:00 a.m. and waited in the rain for three and a half hours …

… IN ORDER TO BE AT THE PAPAL AUDIENCE IN ST. PETER'S SQUARE TO SEE … PAPA FRANCESCO! Pope Francis!

Finally, the Pope Mobile was coming down the side aisle from St. Peter's Basilica and started to turn in front of us. Scott held Ave up in the air, like Simba in the Lion King. The Head of the Secret

Service came and took her from Scott and held her up to the Holy Father. It seemed like a dream when Pope Francis started talking to Scott, asking her name and her age, and then he blessed and kissed her and blessed us all. What an amazing gift it was to see the Holy Father up close! He is so warm, friendly, and you can tell he is fed by being among the people. This was obviously an experience we will never forget!

Fast forward to one month later.

We are back home in Phoenix and it is time for our cardiologist appointment.

We meet with the doctor to hear our results from her cardiology appointment:

One hole closed!

The second one is half the size and shrinking! Our little miracle!

Praise God! We believe that Pope Francis blessed us with this miracle!

Lyn Cassidy is married to Scott and has three children, ages 20, 17 and 4, the youngest of whom has DS. They live in Phoenix, AZ, and are looking forward to having Ave attend Catholic school soon!

Being Inclusive Benefits All

National Catholic Board on Full Inclusion

Today begins National Inclusive Schools Week!! Hooray!

To start off our week of profiling amazing inclusive Catholic schools, we are sharing the words of one of our inclusion mentors, Susan Rinaldi, from Bishop O'Connell High School, about what it is like to work in an inclusive Catholic setting:

"I am blessed to be working with two wonderful special-education teachers who have their masters degrees, are young, and incredibly capable. However, we consider all teachers that work with our students to be part of our team, and ultimately the whole school. I have the privilege of working with many fantastic teachers at O'Connell who have completely embraced, and taken on the responsibility for teaching students receiving expanded services. They inspire me with their innovation, thoughtfulness, and eagerness. I have a freshman student with Down syndrome who is quiet and introverted, but she is learning French. The teacher is amazing. We work with a world geography teacher who is teaching three very different students receiving expanded services. He lights up when he shares his plan for differentiating a given lesson for each student.

He seeks our input, but his instructional strategies are spot on. These are only two examples of many, not to mention the peer mentors who rise to the occasion, go above and beyond what is expected and blow my mind continually."

As you can see, this kind of experience is transformative for everyone involved. We say this a lot but we will say it again, BEING INCLUSIVE BENEFITS EVERYONE...teachers, whose ability to teach gets better, typical students, who lose the discomfort of disability and have the joy of truly standing in the margins and seeing the humanity and sacred holiness in every person, the institution, which has the chance to actually live Catholic Social Teachings on campus every single day, the students with disabilities, who are no longer marginalized and are seen as FULL participants in their community, and the families, who have the joy of building an engaged and committed Catholic school.

Inclusive Catholic schools are possible and worth every effort.

#letsdothis #sayyes #inclusionmatters #siblingstogether #faithandfamily

By: National Catholic Board on Full Inclusion Facebook post/Beth Foraker

Saying YES

Abigail Greer

"Yes" is the most important word you can say to a family. There is such power in a letter of acceptance for all students. Over the course of my career, I've been able to facilitate some very unique "yes" opportunities for families. It was so empowering and uplifting to say "yes" to a student when they have been told "no" before.

By saying "yes" to a student who may have different needs, you are giving your school community the opportunity to learn and grow in a ways that you cannot replicate. Inclusion positively impacts all members of a school community, we know this anecdotally and it is also backed by research. But, the moments of empathy, kindness and happiness that are created can not be measured. I am thankful for the families who have trusted us with their perfectly-made children and have said "yes" back!

Abigail Greer is the Director of Student Service at Bishop McNamara High School. She is the parent of 2 and has spent her entire career in Catholic education

We Wanted a Catholic Education for Michael

Susan Schuller

Truly the deepest, most paralyzing fear I felt when Michael was born and we were told he had DS, was that he would never truly be loved or accepted outside of our family. Dan and I were grateful that we had four other children that could help us build a wall of protection for him. We were intensely afraid. We even delayed telling some close family members because we knew, "They like things perfect."

Imagine how parents feel who have a prenatal diagnosis and have not even yet met their child. The bombardment of pro-abortion information and pressure that is given to them directly and indirectly by the medical community, and even their family and friends is, at best, saddening. It is no wonder that between 70–92% of babies with a prenatal diagnosis of Down syndrome are aborted in the US today.

I never dreamed that Michael would be at a Catholic school with his siblings because to me that would have been ridiculous. I thought that you needed specially trained people to directly teach someone with intellectual disabilities. Michael taught me differently. But I was still gaining the courage to ask Mrs. Kopas, our principal, whom I had known for several years, to allow Michael to be at GCS.

The public school refused to teach him his letters. If they hadn't refused to teach him, I likely would not have had the courage to make the request to Mrs. Kopas. I knew the public school was wrong, but ultimately, I realized God was calling us to put Michael at GCS.

My desire then to have Michael at GCS was driven by three thoughts:

1. I wanted Michael to have God as an integral part of his day and to learn about his faith and be taught the curriculum alongside his peers, just like I wanted for my other children.

2.   I knew what Michael had done for our family and I wanted that benefit to spread to all of the other families at GCS that we so loved.

3.   I wanted to help spread respect, understanding, acceptance, and appreciation of differences so that these students would have a better perspective than I did after twelve years of Catholic schooling and never knowing anyone with Down syndrome or any disability.

Our Catholic faith tells us that we are to accept whatever we are given in terms of an unborn child and to respond in trust, by choosing life. Honestly, I have an extremely difficult time with the disconnect that when it is time for the child to enter school, some children are not welcome. Many schools will simply turn children with special needs away. It breaks my heart and makes me question my faith when I hear of this happening.

Trust me, I am not an unrealistic Pollyanna. I don't think it is easy or that the right supports are already in place.

But in forty years, it should have become more of a priority for our Catholic schools to try to problem solve and work to include all children into our Catholic schools.

It takes incredible courage for a parent to even ask! Any time a parent selects to place their child in a situation that is not inherently set up to specifically deal with their child's challenges, they are exposing themselves to a situation that could easily result in embarrassment or ridicule. It is hard. The parent relies on the mercy of someone they may not even know for their child to even be considered at that school.

I know inclusion, when done right, will create a bigger group of people willing to include all people with special needs into their lives, throughout their lives—including them into their neighborhoods, into friendships, and into their parish communities. I hope this will continue even into employment time because they played side by side, worked next to each other, and collaborated together. I get to see on a daily basis that you CAN change the world by reaching one heart at a time.

~~~~~~

Susan Schuller is the mom of six children, the fifth of whom has DS. So grateful for all of the champions in our lives who support us and meaningful inclusion.

Characterized by Compassion and Care

Patricia McGann

I think we can all agree that the admissions process we employ when we are working with parents of children with special needs must be a process that is characterized by compassion and care. Can you imagine how difficult it is for the parent who calls our school seeking a safe place to land for his disabled child, for his family? How many times did he begin to dial and then hang up the phone? Where did he find the courage to ask for acceptance from strangers in a world that shuns that child daily? Our response to that first call is not just a "secretary's" response, or a "school's" response. At that moment, we speak for our Church. What do we say, and how do we say it? Before we ask parents to complete an often complicated and expensive application process, we take the extra time and effort to talk and to listen.

We don't say, "We don't have the resources to teach your child." We don't suggest that public school is the preferred option for children with special needs. We don't ask for an IEP or testing before we have ever laid eyes on a child. We treat this family with compassion. At the same time, we take care not to mislead families, and we take care to be sure we have enough information to make a reasoned decision about whether or not we can provide a child with a meaningful educational experience. This part is harder. This is the part where we must suspend our need to know that a child will learn how to read fluently or multiply and divide. This is the time when we must focus on the needs of the child rather than our own need to be sure. All the assessments in the world cannot predict that a child with special needs will benefit from the instruction we provide. They can direct instruction, classroom placement, and scheduling, but they only present a piece of the picture of the child before us. We must take care to hold hope for the family – to begin by asking, "What can we do to make this school work for this child?"

Don't be reluctant to invite parents to take a tour of the school and meet with the principal. During that first meeting the goal is to find out what they are looking for for their family. Ask open-ended questions, encouraging parents to express their hopes for their child, and describe their family. This interview can allow you to travel at least a short part of a difficult journey with this family, and maybe even make that journey a little easier for them. If, however, your focus is on convincing them that you cannot serve their child, you will surely add one more heartache to their lives.

Simply ask, "Tell me about _____", and you will find that most parents focus first on labels and diagnoses. To redirect the conversation, you might simply say, "Tell me all the good things about_____", or "Tell me what she likes to do." Ask directly, "What are you hoping to find here at our school?", and you will get a good sense of who these parents are and what they need. You won't know whether or not you can meet their need, but you have accomplished two important things in your first meeting. You have allowed the parents the opportunity to make their case for inclusion, and you have gotten enough information to know what you need to know next.

Schedule a family visit. The Resource Director/Teacher will meet with the child and his or her siblings. At the same time, you will meet with the parents to review the testing they have sent you since their last visit. By then you will have reviewed the testing with the Resource Teacher, and you have a good idea of what supports this child will need to be successful in your school. After this visit, meet with your Resource Teacher to decide on admission. Ask yourselves, "What can we do to make this work for this child and for his future classmates and teachers?"

The must haves before you make a decision:

- Confidence that you and the parents can agree to be partners in the education of their child.

- Confidence that teachers and parents will be able to communicate candidly ensuring that this child can be successful in school.

- Confidence that all students in the class will have access to outstanding instruction and appropriate support as they navigate the school year.

- Confidence that you have explored options such as placement in another class, or flexible scheduling.

- Confidence that you can and will provide teachers with necessary ongoing professional development with respect to inclusion and specifically for the needs of this child.

- Courage, and commitment to make your school a school that values the gifts and needs of all children and families.

God sends the families of children with special needs our way for a reason. With compassion and care you will make the right decision. When you decide to accept a child with special needs, arms wide open, you will not only change his or her life, you will change the lives of every person in your school

"Ask Jesus what he wants from you, and be brave!" –Pope Francis

Patricia McGann former principal at Our Lady of Lourdes Catholic School, Bethesda MD.
Article printed in NCEA 2017. Published with permission.

Starbucks and Abby

Mimi Gehres

My example of inclusion in our Catholic school experience is a very subtle one.

After twelve years in the public school system, we made the difficult decision to pull our daughter out and try something different. We enrolled our daughter in a Catholic all-girls high school that demonstrated a real commitment to inclusive education for young women with intellectual disabilities.

We felt optimistic that Abby would be embraced and respected, but we couldn't have anticipated just how typical her days would become. The favorite example came one afternoon when I came to pick Abby up after school. She had asked me before school that morning if she and one of her friends from her cohort could go to Starbucks after school. I told her of course, I was happy to drive them. To my surprise, when she exited the building with this friend, a large group of girls were following along.

I assumed at first that these girls were just being nice and walking with the girls towards their cars but much to my surprise, one by one they all piled in. I was both a little alarmed and amused because I didn't know who these girls were! But what more common experience for a teenage girl than to invite a bunch of friends to go to a Starbucks after school!

At first, I was a little concerned that maybe they were just along for the ride, but it became clear in listening to their conversations that they were truly interested in my daughter. Listening to them singing along to the music that Abby requested me to play on the radio and listening to the interactions, it became clear that I was in for a very different type of experience at this school. These girls didn't see her as different than anyone else they went to school with, so of course when she invited them to Starbucks they were more than happy to join.

Once we arrived at Starbucks they were all very much like every other teenage girl in that shop. My daughter and her friend from her cohort and all the other "typical" girls were sitting at tables talking about their day, laughing about funny things that happened at school or over the summer and just enjoying each other's company for a brief respite before the homework started. Once we finished at Starbucks that day, I wondered if she would ever hear from those girls again or if it was just a fleeting moment? But I heard about those girls over and over again throughout the year. All of them attended her sweet sixteen birthday party and celebrated her and enjoyed her. They talk to her in the hallways and say hello when I see them. Thiswas the most refreshing, honest, and subtle experience of inclusion I've ever had and it may have been one of the most meaningful.

Mimi Gehres is the mother of Abigail (16) and Roman (13). She and her husband, Ed, feel blessed by both children and the opportunity to give Abby such an inclusive experience at Holy Cross Catholic School. They live in Maryland.

Why Inclusion Is Important to Me

Anne Dillon

Patience. A word many people say about me when they find out I am a special education teacher. I hear, "You must have so much patience." My husband, who has known me since high school, chuckles. "Anne is the last person with any patience." This is true; however, let me clarify that my lack of patience is not in waiting my turn or giving another person the time they need. My impatience is different. Working with students with disabilities for the majority of my career, I have patience to break down a concept, to differentiate a lesson, and to understand the needs of my students. I lack patience with the things that impede progress for learners or create barriers to their growth. That is where I will never have patience.

Education transforms lives. My parents encouraged education. They instilled in me and my siblings that we could do anything we wanted if we were educated. Education meant different things to me and my siblings. We took different paths but found successful careers.

I am one of eight children. I fall about as middle of the pack as one can be. We all went to Catholic school. I have no idea how my parents afforded this, but they made it happen. We attended our parish school in Maryland. All of us attended except for one. My brother Michael was not allowed to go to school with us. This reason had nothing to do with the school being Catholic, for Mike had no public school to attend either. The laws didn't exist at the time to allow people with a disability to have an education.

Mike is four years older than me. He was diagnosed with an intellectual disability. When he was younger, there were limited resources to help Mike or to guide my parents. Growing up, we all played together and did the typical sibling stuff like jumping on the bed or throwing the ball around. We didn't treat Mike any differently, but we knew Mike had challenges. Mike didn't talk. He loved to listen to music and still does. He loved to swing on the swings. As we grew older, he had trouble keeping up with us. Sometimes he got upset with loud noises or when conversations got heated. With so many kids in the house, this obviously happened often. My parents always said Mike had a special place in heaven and that we should learn from him.

I was always bothered that Mike couldn't go to school with us. It just wasn't fair. I believed he could learn so much with us if he could just be given that opportunity. Unfortunately, there were no opportunities at the time. The idea of inclusion simply didn't exist.

I remember sitting at my desk in second grade. I loved my teacher. I remember thinking I was going to be a teacher one day. A few years later, I realized I wanted to teach students like Mike. Special education laws hadn't been passed yet nor did I even have a name for this type of education. I just knew I would be a teacher for kids like Mike.

When I started high school, I became aware of programs providing opportunities for people with disabilities. I volunteered wherever I could. Although Mike was an adult at this point, a few programs became available. Michael had a place to go that provided structure, learning, and social interactions. Sadly, these programs were not inclusive nor were they designed to even consider inclusion.

Eventually, I was employed with the public school system as a special education teacher. It was an amazing experience. Although my school was a separate school at the time, I was tasked in transitioning students back to their neighborhood school. It was my first step into inclusive education. I quickly recognized that my students' grades improved when learning side by side with their peers. I observed behavioral changes and positive social interactions as expectations were set high. It was a win-win! Decades later, the research clearly confirms that inclusive education works. It is what all of our students need.

I was delighted when I received a call from a Catholic high school seeking a resource teacher. At that time, I was working in central office and had enough years to retire. I was thrilled to go to a Catholic school and work directly with students again. The program was designed to support students with high incidence disabilities. The beauty of this program was that this school did not have any legal obligation to provide an education to students with disabilities. Ethically, yes, we are all God's children and are expected to serve them, but legally, no. It was an amazing experience. I was appointed a director position and moved the program to being even more inclusive. Prior to my leaving for a new position elsewhere, the school made a commitment to develop a program for students with intellectual disabilities. There are very few inclusive programs for students with intellectual disabilities at the high school level. This was very exciting! I get emotional when I think about this. My brother Mike would have had a place to learn.

In the next few weeks, I will be embarking on a role that will allow me to promote inclusion in Catholic elementary schools. There are many Catholic schools that provide an education to students with all ability levels. Of course, we need to increase that. Again, I get emotional about this because it brings me full circle with my brother. If we could rewind the decades and Mike could attend school with us, I can only imagine how amazing that would have been for all of us.

Today, Mike is doing very well. He lives in a neighborhood a few counties away with roommates he has known for over twenty years. Mike is happy. As my parents always said, Mike has his place in heaven and we can learn from him. When I look at Mike, I see love, I see goodness. I see God.

Inclusion is so incredibly important in every aspect of our lives. It provides us with opportunities to interact with people who may be different from us. I am not just referring to people with disabilities, but to all people. As a parent, my children had to invite everyone in their class to their parties. We didn't exclude. As an adult, I find myself drawn to people who are different from me. There is so much to learn and so much to give. Inclusion in our Catholic schools connects with our Christian values and is ultimately a social justice issue. Jesus says, "Let the children come to me, and do not prevent them; for the kingdom of heaven belongs to such as these." Jesus would not turn the children away, nor should we. Inclusion is important to me from a very deep personal level. My goal is to see inclusion as the norm and not the exception. Remember, I really don't have much patience, so I need to get busy!

Anne Dillon is a lifelong special educator who continues to promote inclusion. She lives in Maryland with her husband and loves spending time with her family, especially her grandson Jaime.

Actions in Alignment at St Gregory's

Paulette Clagon

We have always been a welcoming community, but it wasn't until the summer of 2017 did we realize that our actions must be in alignment with our mission statement:

St. Gregory the Great School fosters a caring Catholic Christian environment, which provides a faith community and challenging curriculum. As a result, each student will recognize their ability and be able to take on a positive role in our society.

The first time we had to focus on the words "caring Catholic Christian" was when a little boy named Nicholas, a first grader, came through the school doors screaming and clinging to his mom.

Thoughts went through my head, "Oh, what am I going to do? How is this going to work? How would his behavior affect the environment of the classroom?"

Like most new situations, you must allow time to take care of things.

I knew our prayer had to be, "I trust you, God."

We had to rely on our faith community, the teachers, and the entire staff. We had to trust that everyone in the building would be the kind of person who would give care to Nicholas and welcome him.

I had to allow God to do his work in helping Nicholas to recognize his ability.

Nicholas is on the spectrum, ASD. His verbal ability was almost non-existent. He had deep anxiety in separating from his mother.

Our beginning strategy was to continue accepting Nicholas into the school each day with his mother sitting in the classroom. This continued for five weeks of our summer session. When summer was over we all exhaled.

At the beginning of the new school year, we weren't sure what to expect. Mom once again had to walk him into the classroom every day where she would sit for a little while. In the beginning, it was very difficult because he would scream "bloody murder." It was doubly hard because mom would cry, too. We slowly began to wean her away from Nicholas and soon the crying began to subside. Things were happening in the classroom that began to transform Nicholas.

His classmates saw something special in Nicholas. Some of them would sit with him in class and give him gentle prompts to stay on task. His classmates became the caring and compassionate students that we knew they would be! In early fall, Nicholas' teacher began to discover some things about his academic ability. She began to realize that though he wasn't confident enough yet to speak, he definitely understood some first-grade concepts. His teacher began to work with him one-on-one after school. Nicolas showed slow and steady progress!

Sometime in the spring, it was decided that it would be better if mom brought Nicholas in after the regular bell. She would walk him down the hallway, but she was able to leave him without incident. Before long she only had to walk him to the front door of the school and he would walk all the way to the back of the school by himself. He knew the routine now. He would unpack his book bag, put his homework folder in the correct place and settle in for the morning routine. At this point, he still wasn't acknowledging anyone at the front office, not making eye contact, and not greeting people. But we were happy with his progress. He was working in class, had made friends, and was playing tag his own way with his classmates.

It just kept getting better! Nicholas participated in the spring musical. His mother and dad said he was singing all the songs all the time at home. He was able to follow stage directions and learned all the cues for the production. He had a blast!

Though Nicolas still prefers to come into school after everyone has gone to class, he now speaks to everyone. Our hearts just melted when he greeted some of the staff by name. Nicholas is a happy student. His learning is amazing. We are still figuring out his interests, but it has been remarkable watching him grow. His mom and dad are grateful to our school community. They have seen the dramatic changes in Nicholas.

"It's time for us to prioritize and infuse our schools with more joy, connection, and a focus on well-being." "Learning will deepen, academic achievements will improve, and we'll raise a generation of happier, well-adjusted, and creatively confident people."- Habib

Paulette Clagon, M.A., Ed, is a Catholic School educator and administrator in the LA Archdiocese for thirty-seven years. She works to transform her community into an inclusive environment.

Creating a True Partnership

Patricia McGann

Essential to successful inclusion is an understanding and acceptance of the particularly Catholic notion that each of us is made in the "image and likeness of God." Catholic schools have historically been safe havens for children, places where children are treated gently and guided carefully as they develop academically, socially, physically, and spiritually.

School leaders who see the children and not the labels create successful inclusive schools. School leaders who commit themselves to unconditional acceptance of children with differences, of teachers who will struggle and fail, and of parents who will be afraid, can and do lead truly inclusive schools.

Parents of children with special learning needs are asking the same thing of us that all parents who seek Catholic education ask. They want to partner with us to see the face of God in their children, provide their children with an excellent education, and help them lead their children to Heaven.

Partnership with parents of children with significant disabilities is even more important to the successful inclusion school. Parents need to be able to trust administrators and teachers to see the potential in their children. They are often afraid to share "too much" information, worrying that school personnel will lower the bar of expectations for their children, or even that their children might be considered "unsuitable" for the school.

One great way to strengthen communication between teachers and administrators and parents is to share a document called a Strengths and Strategies Profile. Teachers complete the form when they have finished the school year with a child and use it for communication with the child's next teachers. More importantly, though, parents can complete the form based on what they see and do at home. If the document is a shared Google doc, then everyone can see all comments and all entries. Transparency and focus on the child create a true partnership!

We can ease the process of inclusion in our schools if we work together and share what we know. If we share our victories and our failures we will see that inclusive education is messy, full of challenges and tears, and incredibly beautiful.

~~~~~~

Patricia McGann is the former principal at Our Lady of Lourdes, Bethesda MD.

Recognizing Others as Children of God

FIRE Foundation

As a Catholic school student, it was not until seventh grade that I fully realized the impact of the FIRE Foundation. It was then that I knew that I would be paired with a first grade buddy. I was really excited to be paired with such a sweet and very cute little girl. It amazed me how much joy her warm smile and tug at the legs made me feel. I have known her family and the thought of her not being part of our school family really saddens me. She has made a lasting impact on me.

I will never forget her and the value of the FIRE Foundation that has enabled her to attend school with not only myself, but especially with her many siblings. I will always continue to support the FIRE Foundation because there is no way I could imagine not having the ability to attend Catholic school with all of my family.

She has helped me understand, being with her every day, that all people with disabilities are a shining light and an example of Jesus. They are just like us; they are God's children, too. I have found that they are happier, brighten up everyone's day, and seem holier. As Jesus said, "Let the children come to me."

Furthermore, I've seen that my sister has always been overjoyed to go to Mass and says prayers with reverence.

I have learned to treat all with respect and how to stand up for those who are not treated with respect. Remembering the gifts they have taught me, I will persist in teaching others what I have learned. I am going to allow respecting others, being joyful, and recognizing others as Children of God to guide my path in life; it will keep me heading in the right direction, in the direction towards God and heaven.

(from educator) He has taught others how to include people with disabilities into their lives. He is a really special boy, even when others can't always understand what he does. He doesn't see a boy with a disability or limitations, he sees someone he loves and who loves him back. What happened between two little boys in a classroom broke down prejudices. It had mutual impact and is a mutual admiration. The seed that was planted in the school through FIRE has spread into the greater community. That is how change happens.

Without inclusive education in my life, my years in grade school would not have been as enjoyable ... has taught me to accept everyone no matter who they appear on the outside, not to judge others, and most importantly has given me incredible friendships that will last a lifetime.

Stories submitted by F.I.R.E of Kansas City. Every year students attending schools in the Diocese of Kansas City-St. Joseph submit essays that provide a brief glimpse into their hearts. Through their words, we hear the voices of our most passionate inclusion advocates.

Through these young people's experiences and through the friendships they have formed, the call to include all students, of all abilities, rings loud and clear. Inclusion provides hourly and daily opportunities for all students to live their Catholic faith and celebrate God's gift of life. It's such a blessing and a privilege, as executive director of the FIRE Foundation, to be in the midst of this new generation of inclusion champions. - Lynn Hire executive director.

Our Journey with Pete

Maggie Keane

A year before I was to graduate from medical school, I was in a serious car accident. I had a stroke and a traumatic brain injury and doctors honestly didn't know what my outcome would be. John and I had been married just two years. After being in ICU for two weeks and rehab hospital for three weeks more, we decided to move back home to Minnesota to live with my parents. Eventually I was able to go back to Creighton University in Nebraska and graduate a year later. It was during that year that we started going to a Baptist-type Catholic Church in Omaha. There was an amazing priest named Father Fangman who talked about how God's graces are the little things some people call coincidences. He said they are actually everywhere and the more you're open to them, the more you'll see.

When John and I moved to Phoenix, we rented a place close to the hospital where I was doing my training. We woke up on one of the first Sunday mornings and heard church bells out our window. They were coming from a church across the street, St. Francis Xavier. We've been going ever since, despite moving a distance away.

Then fast forward 10 years and three boys later. Our third son, Pete, was born with Down syndrome. We were still attending SFX, and now our older boys were attending school there, too. We had heard previously from other families that children with special needs were not able to be accepted at SFX, so our hearts grew heavy with worry. It was our dream for all of our boys to attend Catholic school together. When Pete was about one year old, we got an email from the principal of SFX, where our older two sons attended. She told us that she felt called to have the school move to total inclusion because of Pete and another SFX family who had a little girl with Down syndrome just a year after Pete. In her email she said that she had brought this idea to the Diocese of Phoenix at a principals' meeting and they all agreed to move to full inclusion. Both John and I broke down with tears of joy! Her email was a huge God's grace to us and our family!!

My husband, John, and I were 99% sure we wanted Pete to join his older two brothers at St, Francis Xavier, but we also wanted what was best for him. Pete would be the first student with Down syndrome at the school, and we felt completely overwhelmed by that thought. We toured the public-school options before the Christmas break, which offered physical, occupational, and speech therapy. But the majority of his day would be spent in a self-contained classroom, a classroom with no windows. We left feeling that God was calling us to take this "leap of faith" with our Catholic school.

This journey has made us pray hard and really trust that God has us and Pete right where he wants us.

Now, how do we find an aide! Being the first, we had no clue where to start, but then God sent us an angel.

She just "happened" to be standing next to my friend after school at SFX the day we had toured the public school programs for Peter. My heart was so twisted because SFX said they would accept Pete, but they did not have an aide or any of the services the public school offered. I poured my heart out to this woman and my friend, telling them of my turmoil and uncertainty. I had no idea that this "angel" standing next to my friend had just moved with her four sons to the school, had a master's degree in special education, and had been wanting to get back into working. After hearing my story, she felt "called" to apply to be Pete's aide. Talk about a God's grace! God does provide!!

We have decided to start Peter at SFX this fall in the preschool class. We think this would be a good transition year for him so he can get some of the routine down, but still have a lot of "play time." This also gives him another year to mature, grow, and get potty trained before starting Kindergarten.

We are scared, but grateful and excited!

The emotions are overwhelming when we let them take over.
We try to be faithful.
We try to walk the path God is leading us on.

Maggie Keane is happily married and mom to four crazy, fun-loving boys. She is a loving Catholic mom and doctor and hopes that a wave of inclusion is starting to happen in Catholic schools,

Our Catholic Story

Michelle and Stacy Tetschner

In the summer of 2014, after a lot of soul searching, my husband and I decided it was time for us to try Catholic school. We were worried. Our principal at our public school was leaving and we knew that we were in for some uphill challenges to keep our son fully included in the public school, so we hoped that we could find a Catholic school that would accept our son. Our older boys had attended Catholic school, so we thought we would find a way to make it happen. We assumed that Catholic schools would be open and accepting of all children. We knew inclusion in Catholic schools was starting to happen around the country. We were ready to find a school in Phoenix and fit the pieces of the puzzle together. We had the money and the resources—we could help them make this work! They should be open to embracing him for who he is, perfectly imperfect!

But sadly, that is not the experience we had. Two schools wouldn't even return our phone call.

We were told no by two other schools.

Then the fifth school principal emailed back and said she would be open to discussing the idea but was leaving on vacation the next day. I emailed back immediately and said that we would be in her office at 1:00 p.m, if she'd meet with us! She agreed!

We were so nervous, so worried! Our hearts were going to break if she also told us no. Our faith had been tested by those four refusals. We didn't know if we could continue to be Catholic if they couldn't accept my son.

We met with her for an hour. We prayed together, we cried, and we had honest conversations. We stated clearly that we knew our son wouldn't be at grade level and she looked so relieved at that statement! We agreed that independence, socialization, and then academics were our goals. We had honest conversations about her expectations of us as parents. We said we would be there to help answer questions about how he learns best, to help with how best to include him, and be available to do a presentation for the students to ask questions. We said we would pay for the aide ourselves and agreed on a salary. We said we would help where she needed us and be on whatever committee she needed us to be on!

We all agreed that we would give it a try!

The first few weeks were challenging for sure. There was a lot of uncertainty and a lot of fear from staff and even the students. This was new to them, they weren't sure how to do inclusion, and we all know: teachers never EVER want to fail.

Our teacher that first year was amazing. Her heart was open and because of her- the class openly accepted my son. I was a room mom, so I could be at school often to help and learn the kids' names and families. This allowed me to reach out to moms to have play dates and do social things with the students that showed friendship to my son.

Everyone gradually began to accept Raymond and see that he absolutely could keep up with the other students and that he was just a kid who wanted to make people laugh, and be included. While he would obviously learn a bit slower and things would need to be modified for him—guess what, he was out of his desk like a shot to go play on the playground, he was always ready for lunch and snack and he was the first one to the locker room to change for PE!

There were things that he was good at and then there were things he needed help with. He was great at small-group science doing hands-on projects, but vocab and complex concepts could be harder to teach. School wasn't without bumps, no journey is, but there weren't any boulders that threw us off course. Slowly we settled in, and Raymond began making friends and opening people's hearts.

Raymond loved going to school every single day. He made friends that we still keep in touch with, he made huge academic progress, and he grew so much that first year! It was amazing. Their expectations were that he keep up with the other students, with help. This was such a refreshing concept, compared to the public schools that said he should be segregated.

This would be my advice to parents: ASK!

Ask if there is room in their heart to include your child.

Principals: find parents, SEEK them out, and ask them if they're willing to take the journey with you.

Inclusion will change your entire school foundation and mission statement. It changes your thought processes.

It creates kindness, patience, and empathy within your school, just as Jesus would have wanted!

We are all one family, God's family. Let's include all!

Michelle and Stacy Tetschner

Section 3: Resources

8 Resolutions for the
2018 Inclusive Classroom

Sean Smith

1. Identify Barriers and Eliminate Them

Barriers to learning exist. They may be part of the school's adopted curriculum or something in the physical classroom setting. Identify these barriers and then eliminate them to alter the learning experience for all students. Reflect on the barriers in your classroom. A few examples of barriers with solutions include:

Weekly spelling list: Provide multiple means of practice so the student is not concentrating on handwriting. Ex: type, dictate, practice with partner, tactile practice (practicing spelling with shaving cream or sand).

Struggling readers needing support with fluency and comprehension: Use digital books, text to speech (audio representation application), visuals representing ideas, and tools that alter reading Lexile levels.

Brainstorming before a writing task: Interactive graphic organizers allow learners to generate ideas through visuals, images, color, shapes, text, and other media. Favorite interactive graphic organizers include:

Inspiration and Kidspiration: Available as software and application; easy-to-create learning webs.

Popplet: Available as a website and application; images, text, and video are added with a "click" and the web grows.

2. Offer Students a Variety of Ways to Demonstrate Understanding

Multiple choice, vocabulary matching, and essay/quizzes/exams are not meant for all students. Offer them options to demonstrate what they know. Consider assessments that allow variety while providing understanding, creating a digital story book, a brief video, an audio podcast, a poster, or a simple cartoon. While we may not be able to replace traditional assessments, we can mix and match formats for learner variability. In this way, you can gauge understanding, engage your learners, and make assessment "fun." Unique demonstrations include:

Digital Story Books: Includes text, images, audio, and more with Story Bird, Pictello, Tar Heel Reader, and Slide Story.

Movie Creation: Direct a movie with iMovie, Filmora, Power-Director, and Quik.

Interactive Slideshows: Develop and share a slideshow with Google Slides, Prezi, Animoto, and Kizoa.

3. Know What's Happening at Home

Sure, we all communicate with our students' home environments. Some of us use a weekly email, create a newsletter that offers updates, or utilize parent conferences to share needed information. Others might look to catch parents at drop-off and pick-up. Maybe you do a combination of these to ensure information on classroom events, activities, and assignments are shared with the home environment. But is this primarily a one-way street? Simply information dissemination?

Use tools that promote two-way communication, allowing parents to report happenings at home. A Google doc can facilitate ongoing interaction to report important events, challenges, and successes. Perhaps it is a repository for posting completed assignments, accessing various classroom resources, asking questions, or offering suggestions. Communication tools include:

- ClassDojo Messenger: Allows teachers to send messages, offer updates, share moments, and extend the classroom culture to an online classroom community.

- EduBlogs: Offer an interactive web presence of posting messages, stories, video, images, and so much more. Parents and students can offer comments and ideas or archive threads for future reference.

- Seesaw: Offers parents a window into the school day. While students document learning, teachers assess and organize it, making it available to families allowing for seamless communication.

- Understand what families and students are experiencing with Understood, an online space developed for families of students with learning and attention issues. The site is filled with ideas and strategies for the classroom and home.

4. Learn Something New Because You Want To, Not Because You Have To

Learning is a continuous process, and professional requirements often find us enrolled in a course or workshop. Continuing education credits and courses are always helpful, but don't forget about *just-in-time* learning. Consider the growing digital resources at your fingertips. Just-in-time learning sites include:

Autism Internet Modules: Developed for educators and parents that offer an array of learning modules for ideas and application including supports for the classroom, workplace, early learning, and general community.

IRIS Center: Offers case studies, downloadable resources, presentations, and more all tied to evidence-based practices for ALL learners, particularly those with disabilities.

Intervention Central: A plethora of resources, just-in-time lessons, professional learning, and interventions to support learning, behavior, and social emotional development.

5. Integrate Technology with Instructional Practices

The growth in technology tools, particularly applications, can be overwhelming. Don't worry about staying on top of each and every app; instead, identify a tech tool that supports the area of instruction you are concentrating on or looking to reinforce or improve. A few ideas include:

- Google's Voice-to-Text Chrome App: Helps the limited typist or writer.

- Co:Writer Universal: Facilitates sentence fluency and writing quantity with its word prediction.

- WatchKnowLearn: Offers a library of video for all subjects, ages, and grades.

- Digital story books: Allow the creation of modified versions of critical resources while simultaneously offering student demonstration of knowledge through a structured, organized format.

- BrainPop and BrainPop Junior: Introduce a variety of standard-based ideas with Tim and Moby through a visual interactive introduction that formulates understanding.

- Newsela: Provide a library of content with an adjustable reading level to differentiate for all learners.

6. Work on the Power of 2 or Maybe 10

Get further connected to access classroom information. Utilize Facebook, Twitter, or Pinterest to follow fellow educators, professionals, or parents who post instructional ideas and ways to further engage our learners. It's amazing what 280 characters and periodic checks (maybe once a week) offer in strategies. Or go old school and join a listserv to obtain daily or weekly updates.

Classroom strategies can be found on:

- Edutopia: Provides tips and strategies flavored with technology and tools that feature ideas directly from the classroom and teachers.

- Pinterest: Offer creative ideas for more than interactive bulletin boards. Find reading activities, ways to engage challenging students, and much more from the educational community.

- Twiducate: Offers a safe social media closed platform to provide teachers and students a place to extend learning outside of the classroom. It also doubles as a social networking site that is safe for students and can be monitored by school and home.

- Did you say Quiet or QIAT? An organization seeking to facilitate the consideration and use of technology for struggling students offers a QIAT List- a virtual community to obtain answers to a range of tech related issues.

7. Look to Unplug

What? Isn't this contrary to Resolution #6? Reconsider the social media that occupies part of your day or week looking for resources that takes you down that rabbit hole. Disconnect from resources that are overwhelming and offer too much information not applicable to your classroom. This might include the myriad of email lists you have subscribed to that clutter your in-box with lesson plan ideas, instructional strategies, and links to websites that you simply do not have time to consider, and yet, feel guilty about not reviewing. Simply unplug from these resources. They make you feel as if you are not doing enough or offer the just-in-time information or solution that you can't apply tomorrow. Identify the social media and digital time zappers and simply unplug.

8. Create an Active Learning Space

Explore ways to further involve your students in their own learning. Give them a voice in how they learn and options available to demonstrate understanding. Let them be decision makers by offering a variety of options. Urge students to align learning to real issues relevant to their community, their future, or ideas that impact them and the broader family and community. Use instructional materials that push students while supporting them with structured "guard rails." Encourage experiences that promote movement in the learning process, reinforcing engagement with peers, educators, and the broader community.

Sean Smith (This material was originally written for the Program for Inclusive Education at the University of Notre Dame's Alliance for Catholic Education.) Published with permission

Meet Sadie
Resources and Who Said That?

Michelle Brooks

Meet Sadie, a bright and energetic 5-year old about to start kindergarten. Sadie loves swing sets, all things princess, and playing fetch with her dogs just like most girls her age. When Sadie was 4 years old, she knew her alphabet, colors, and could sight read 50+ words. Sadie lives across the street from a neighborhood elementary school and yet, unlike her peers, she is not allowed to attend this school with the neighborhood kids. Instead, her parents have been advised to put her in a self-contained classroom for kindergarten and be bused to another school…which, by the way, will be a different school, every year, for the next 6 years. Why? It's not for behavior issues or because she hasn't been able to show some school readiness. Sadly, it's simply because Sadie has Down syndrome. When her parents asked about inclusion, the school district replied that was not how they do things, nor would they recommend that path for Sadie. Unfortunately, this school is not alone as this is the attitude of many school districts across the nation. Dr. Cathy Pratt, a Board-Certified Behavior Analyst with doctoral training in behavior analysis and the Director of the Indiana Resource Center for Autism, argues that discussing inclusion in terms of student inclusion, inclusive classrooms, or inclusive schools misses the point of inclusion and states, "The philosophy of inclusion encourages the elimination of the dual special and general education systems, and the creation of a merged system that is responsive to the realities of the student population." (Pratt, 1997) This student population Dr. Pratt speaks of does not consist of students with equal abilities, aptitudes, and backgrounds even without adding a child with a disability into the mix. The educational conveyer belt of the past is ineffective and antiquated even for typical students without an Individualized Education Plan (IEP). Thankfully, many educators realize that each student is an individual and every classroom has children with a wide range of strengths and weaknesses and the modern classroom is embracing various strategies to meet the variety of needs. However, there is confusion about what inclusion really is and educators at all levels still fight the idea of welcoming students with disabilities into their general education classrooms. Research shows that inclusion benefits all students because inclusion creates a better learning environment for all, increases empathy and acceptance of differences, and results in greater academic outcomes.

To fully understand inclusion, it is important to understand that the terms "inclusion" and "mainstreaming" are often intermixed in conversations about the educational options of students with special needs, when they are not the same thing. Mainstreaming focuses on a student's readiness for the general curriculum which leads to the principles of separation if a student has special needs. (Bui, Almazan, Quirk, & Valenti, 2010) To the contrary, inclusion is the concept that ALL students can benefit from differentiated instruction and creates a sense of belonging without labels or judgments. Inclusion is not just about including children with disabilities into the general education classrooms, it's about including all students of all abilities and backgrounds. Typical students should have access to all the supports and resources that the special needs student has, and the special needs student should have access to the same general curriculum that the typical student has access to. (Pratt, 1997) All students can learn together in an inclusive environment regardless of labels.

Successful inclusion starts by creating a better learning environment for all. This can begin before the students even arrive to school on the first day of class. The physical classroom environment can either promote learning and student cooperation or distract and impede learning. Teachers can use color, decoration, design, and organizational strategies to make a classroom feel warm and inviting.

(Buchloz & Sheffler, 2009) A cozy pillow in a reading corner is not only practical for encouraging literacy but can be used for the top learners in the class to have a space when they finish assignments early and creates a space for any student struggling that feels overwhelmed and just needs a place to regroup. Desks should be arranged where every student is accessible to the teacher and students are facing the teacher. Decorations should be minimal and classroom books and supplies should be tidy and organized. (Buchloz & Sheffler, 2009) In younger grades, it is helpful to make schedules and classroom procedures visual. Teachers could also consider alternative seating such as yoga ball. In a recent study by the Department of Exercise Science at Elon University, Molly Burgoyne concluded that yoga balls engage the vestibular system and improve sensory processing which results in improved focus and classroom performance. (Burgoyne & Ketcham, 2015)

In addition to the physical environment, a teacher should build a positive and supportive atmosphere for the students by creating a classroom community that will promote an inclusive learning environment. All students should feel a sense of belonging to the greater community in the classroom and the school. One way this can be done is by establishing classroom traditions and routines. (Buchloz & Sheffler, 2009) It should be noted that if there is to be a change in routine, it would be best to start talking about it well in advance to allow the students time to mentally prepare so they will be able to transition smoothly when the day comes. Another strategy to building a community is to hold classroom meetings to problem solve and teach appropriate social behavior. (National Association of Special Education Teachers, n.d., Buchloz & Sheffler, 2009) Classroom meetings can be a time for learning new skills through role-play and observation, modeling appropriate behavior, social stories, practicing being active listeners and being heard, practicing and showing respect, brainstorming solutions, offering praise, and resolving conflicts. (National Association of Special Education Teachers, n.d.)

Teachers can prepare and establish built in procedures and systems that will contribute to a positive learning environment. Effective inclusive classrooms are proactive in encouraging positive behaviors. Rather than waiting for a behavior issue to develop, teachers can implement behavioral supports from day one. The National Association of Special Education Teachers (NASET) suggest that the most important behavioral intervention strategy is verbal praise and rewards for positive behavior. Behavior systems that focus on negative behaviors often increase the frequency and intensity of unwanted behavior and don't provide the student with the skills needed to behave differently. If a reprimand is in order, the NASET recommends that it's done privately, with a calm voice, and looking at the student without forcing eye contact. (National Association of Special Education Teachers, n.d.)

Secondly, effective inclusion creates empathy and understanding of diversity. Dr. William Henninger IV, an Assistant Professor of Family Studies at the University of Northern Iowa, has focused on inclusion in the preschool setting and claims that the repeated and impromptu opportunities for interactions between typical and disabled peers foster positive attitudes and understanding about disabilities. Dr. Henniger cites a study by Diamond and Hong that shows that typically developing children have demonstrated that they are able to initiate interactions and are able to identify appropriate ways to include and engage fair play with students with disabilities. (Henniger, 2014, Diamond & Hong, 2010) Moreover, there is additional evidence to support that when typical students are given opportunities to model appropriate behavior and be a peer mentor to their peers with special needs, they show an increase in self-esteem, confidence, improved leadership skills and demonstrate academic gains. (Henniger, 2010)

Additionally, Dr. Henniger claims that when children are exposed to individuals with disabilities at an early age, they are less inclined to view disabilities as an impairment and are more likely to approach individuals with differences more confidently and with acceptance throughout their lives. However, it is to be noted that if a typically developed child does not have opportunities at a young age to interact with disabled peers, the older the child is, the less receptive they are to children with disabilities being included in an academic setting. Therefore, early inclusion is a key factor to successful inclusion. (Henniger, 2010)

There are mountains of evidence to support the claims that students with disabilities show greater academic gain in inclusive environments. Sue Buckley, Director of Science and Research and founder of Down syndrome Education International, is one of the foremost authorities on education for individuals with Down syndrome and has spent her life researching best practices and methods for educating individuals with Down syndrome. Dr. Buckley has categorically endorsed inclusion and her research shows significant academic gains for children with Down syndrome in an inclusive general education classroom verses a special education setting. This can be contributed to two factors; the spoken language of the typical peer group provides an engaging learning environment, and the pace of learning is greater. (Buckley, Bird, & Sacks, 2002) As an example, Sue references an included teenager that has daily literacy instruction with his/her typically developing peers. The targets for the lesson will be different for the included student and academic supports will be implemented, within the classroom setting allowing for the typical peers to be role models and ideally, tutors. However, in a special education setting, the teacher has to plan an appropriate literacy for 6 students – two are autistic, two have behavior difficulties and two have Down syndrome – all have significant delays in speech and language and only a few of them can even write their name. Rather than a formal lesson, reading a story together is the more appropriate group activity. Buckley wants to emphasize that this finding is in no way a criticism to special education schools and classrooms and is simply an example to explain their research outcomes. (Buckley et al., 2002) Dr. Carol Quirk, Director of Technical Assistance to Early Intervention Programs in North Carolina, and her team support Buckley's findings as they cite 20 years of research on inclusion and state that there are not any studies since 1970 that have shown any academic advantages for students with disabilities to be educated in a separate classroom or school. (Bui., 2010)

But what about typically developing students? How does inclusion impact their academic progress? Critic of inclusion are concerned that students with special needs, especially those with behavior issues, will cause a reduction in instruction time take away from the general education student's academic experience. Carol Quirk referenced multiple studies that indicated no differences in instructional time in classrooms with a disabled student than a classroom without one. In addition, Dr. Quirk cited research by Waldron, Cole, and Majd (2001) that shows evidence that inclusive classrooms show greater academic gains in math and literacy for the typical student than the non-inclusive classrooms. (Bui et al., 2010, Waldron, Cole, & Majd, 2001) This may be attributed to typical students having unique learning opportunities as they engage, mentor and tutor the student with a disability. This peer support allows students to have higher levels of engagement with the curriculum when they are in that supporting role and the special needs student also benefits by having more time engaged in curriculum activities. These findings challenge the notion that inclusive classrooms take away from general education students. On the contrary, all students benefit from inclusion as research indicates.

In conclusion, research shows that inclusion benefits all students because inclusion creates a better learning environment for all, increases empathy and acceptance of differences, and results in greater academic outcomes. Remember Sadie? Well, Sadie's parents found an alternative school that embraces inclusion. She is nearing the end of her kindergarten year and her teachers report that Sadie is one of the top readers in the class and is thriving in every area. She has been embraced by her peers and their parents and has been invited to birthday parties and other community events. Moreover, Sadie is not the only child with special needs in her class and that student has also shown significant cognitive-social gains as the year has progressed. At the beginning of the year, Jack, a child with severe autism, struggled to adapt to the classroom environment. Yet, with patience, perseverance, and proper supports, he has thrived beyond expectation. The typically developing students in Sadie's class have been supported in their understanding of difficulties and differences and to them, Sadie and Jack are simply their friends. With early inclusion, proper supports and evidence-based practices, inclusion absolutely works.

References:

Bucholz, J. L., & Sheffler, J. L. (2009). Creating a Warm and Inclusive Classroom Environment: Planning for All Children to Feel Welcome, Electronic Journal for Inclusive Education, 2 (4).

Buckley, S, Bird, G, Sacks, B, and Archer, T. (2002) A comparison of mainstream and special education for teenagers with Down syndrome: implications for parents and teachers. *Down syndrome News and Update*, 2(2), 46-54. doi:1,0.3104/updates.166

Bui, X., Almazan, S., Quirk, C., & Valenti, M., (2010). Inclusive education research & practice. Retrieved from http://www.mcie.org/usermedia/application/6/inclusion_works_final.pdf

Burgoyne, M. E., & Ketcham, C. J. (2015). Observation of Classroom Performance Using Therapy Balls as a Substitute for Chairs in Elementary School Children. *Journal of Education and Training Studies*, 3(4), 42-48. doi:10.11114/jets.v3i4.730

Diamond, K.E., & Hong, S.-Y. (2010). Young children's decisions to include peers with physical disabilities in play. Journal of Early Intervention, 32, 163–177.

Henninger, IV, W. R. (2014). How do children benefit from inclusion?. *First steps to preschool inclusion.* (pp. 34-54). Baltimore, MD: Brookes Publishing.

National Association of Special Education Teachers (n.d.). Promoting positive social interactions in an inclusion setting for students with learning disabilities. Retrieved from http://faculty.uml.edu/darcus/01.505/NASET_social_inclusion.pdf

Pratt, C. (1997). There is no place called inclusion. The Reporter, 2(3), 4-5, 13-14.

Waldron, N., Cole, C., & Majd, M. (2001). The academic progress of students across inclusive and traditional settings: A two year study Indiana inclusion study. Bloomington, IN: Indiana Institute on Disability & Community.

Michelle Brooks is a mom to eight children and is a fierce advocate for inclusion for her daughter Sadie. Michelle has gone back to school to get her teaching degree, so she can be part of the solution in creating more opportunities of inclusion in her classroom.

Harmful Effects of Segregation

Carrie Ro

Does Self-Contained Special Deliver on Its Promise?

Studies Shedding Light on the Negative Effects of Educating Children in Self-Contained Classroom

"No child should be denied his or her right to an education in Faith, which in turn nurtures the soul of a nation." –Pope Benedict XVI "

- No educational advantage of a self-contained, segregated classroom, only disadvantages. (Buckley, S.J., Bird, G., Sacks, B. & Archer, T., 2006)

- No academic advantage (Falvey, 2004)

- Inferior quality of IEP goals (Hunt & Farron-Davis, 1992)

- Poorer quality of instruction in academic skills (NCLB, Wheelock, 1992)

- Lack of generalization to regular environments (Stokes & Baer, 1977)

- Disruption of opportunities for sustained interactions and social relationships with typical students (Strully & Strully, 1992)

- Decrease in the confidence that general education teachers have for teaching diverse learners (Giangreco *et al.*, 1993)

- Absence of appropriate role and behavior models (Lovett, 1996)

- Negative impact on classroom climate and student attitudes about differences (Fisher, Sax, & Rodifer, 2000)

- Children with Down syndrome who are educated in special classrooms are more than 2 years behind on expressive language than children with Down syndrome who are fully included (Buckley, *DownsEd*)

- No gains were made in speech and language in the students that were in special classrooms (Buckley, DownsEd)

- No improvements in school achievements (Cuckle, 1998)

- There is no such thing as a self-contained world, educating students in a self-contained room does not allow the students to learn all of the other things they will need to survive in this very large world (Decatur & Bassett, 2007)

- Students who stay their whole career in a self-contained classroom have a 5 percent shot at a diploma. And that is immoral," said the DOE's chief academic officer, Shael Polakow-Suransky. "We cannot allow thousands of kids to be confined to failure."

- Disruption of sustained opportunities for social relationships (Strully & Strully, 1992)

- Disruption of Maslow's Theory that "all human beings need to belong before they can achieve" (Kunc, 1992)

Carrie Ro is happily married and a mom to three children. Her middle son has DS. She is passionate about inclusion and helps families who want to follow an inclusive path for their children. Her primary focus is to open the doors of Catholic schools and get them to see the value and benefits to all students when they embrace and implement an inclusive mindset. She currently resides in Dallas.

Favorite Quotes

"Down syndrome isn't a burden. How people react to it is" Stephanie Holland

"Early segregation does not merely predict later segregation, it almost ensures it." Eric Carter

"When you focus on someone's disability you'll overlook their abilities, beauty ad uniqueness. Once you learn to accept and love them for who they are, you subconsciously learn to love yourself unconditionally" Yvonne Pierre

"Inclusion is
a way of thinking,
a way of being,
and a way of making decisions about helping someone belong."
Julie Causten

"Intelligence is not a one-dimensional construct, nor can it(for its absence) be measured accurately and reliably enough to base students educational programs and future goals on test results" Chery Jorgenson

"Our communities are still struggling to practice a true inclusion, full participation that finally becomes ordinary, normal. This requires not only technical and specific programs, but first of recognitions and acceptance of faces, tenacious and patient confidence that each person is unique and unrepeatable." Pope Francis

"As Catholic schools, if we claim to be pro-life, it means we must be committed to pro-life-span and to teaching all of God's children." Marco Clark

"An education in the fullness of humanity should be the defining feature of the Catholic schools. An inclusive education finds a place for all and does not select in an elitist way the beneficiaries of its efforts". Pope Francis

"Fairness is not giving everyone the same thing; fairness is giving each person what they need to succeed" unknown

"We should assume that poor performance is due to instructional inadequacy rather than to student deficit; in other words, if a student does not do well, the quality of the instructions should be questioned before the students ability to learn" Donnellan 1984

"Children learn best when they feel valued, when people hold high expectations for them, and when they are taught and supported well." Cheryl Jorgenson

"Inclusion is not a strategy to help people fit into the systems and structures which exist in our societies: it is about transforming those systems and structures to make it better for everyone" Diane Richler

"Everyone is born with a treasure chest of gifts and talents that they need to discover and share" Pope Francis

"It is through faith, the power of faith, that we see persons with disabilities, not as a disability to cope with, but as a gift to be with, to treasure and to love" Bishop Emeritus Paul Loverde

"Lets talk about STRONG, not wrong" Cormac Russell

"There comes a moment when you realize that what you're advocating for is more than just accommodations. You're really advocating for someone's quality of life. That's the moment you realize you won't give up." Kelli Sandman-Hurley

"Don't Limit Me!" by Megan Bombaars

"Behavior IS Communication"

"Special Education is a service, not a place"

"Non-Speaking does not mean Non-Thinking"

"See the ABLE, not the LABEL"

IEP 101: Basics for Parents

Carrie Ro, Sarah Lombard, and Michelle Tetschner

1. <u>When:</u> IEPs are typically held once a year in the spring to prep for the next school year. **NOTE: an IEP meeting can be called at any time,** and you can have multiple meetings throughout the year as needed or requested. It's suggested that while spring is a good time to get ready for the next year, a meeting in fall may be a necessity. At that time, you can assess what is and isn't working, you know who the team is, and they can then modify and change the supports and goals as needed just a few weeks into the school year, not losing an entire school year.

2. <u>Who:</u> The IEP team will consist of approximately 5–8 school staff and you. It can be intimidating, so be prepared mentally. **NOTE: Never Go Alone.** Bring your own team with you including your spouse, 1–3 friends, and possibly an advocate or another experienced mom to help balance the numbers at the table. Invite outside therapists to give their expertise in person or at least in a report. Inviting the principal may be a good suggestion.

3. <u>Timeline:</u> Put in writing a request that the draft IEP and all assessments **be received at least forty-eight hours** in advance. This is a MUST. A favorite advocate suggests the draft be given one week in advance, to research your own goals/ideas, add verbiage, write in the parental portion, and return for the team to see your vision and suggestions. **NOTE: This is a legal and binding document.** You need to prep for this meeting. You are the CEO of your child. A lawyer or CEO would never read a document for the first time in front of five other

people, nor should you. Having a draft allows you to read it and bring new ideas and resources to the table. Remember: you know your child best! You are the one with the most knowledge at that table. Be knowledgeable in the strengths of your child, how they learn best and what your goals and visions are. Think BIG—think college!

4. Lead the Meeting: Be the leader. Start the meeting off with an "About Me" handout. Allow the team to see your child outside of school, their interests, involvement in the community, and their strengths. This vision will drive goals. **NOTE: Goals drive services**. What services does your child need to reach your vision? Develop goals that are accountable and specific. Be clear on who works on the goal, when, where and time of day it is being implemented, and how assessments are completed. Example of a poorly written goal: learning the second-grade Dolce words. The team knew there were forty words, but when the month of April came it was realized they had only worked on ten of the words. They stated that until mastery of the first ten words was complete, they couldn't move on. A well-written goal would be: "Mastery of the first 40 second-grade Dolce words with no more than one verbal prompt, with data collected weekly. This would include benchmarks of: 10 words by October, 20 words by December, 30 words by April, 40 words by May, with 80% accuracy"—much more clear, concise, and accountable. Be clear and concise. **NOTE: You can record the meeting**. Some states may require advance notice to record. Recording it is a suggested common practice.

5. Be the resource of the resource: if they need it, you can find it. If they need ideas on how best to teach reading, you can bring suggested reading programs for children with Down syndrome. Bring accommodations and modification suggestions

to the team that your child may need. **NOTE: not all children will learn alike; not all children with Down syndrome are the same.** While phonics may work for children in general, many children with Down syndrome do better with "whole word" or the Fast Flash method. Keep in mind that teachers may not have worked with a child with Down syndrome before. They may be fearful and worried. Assure them that you are a team; you are there to help, to support, and most of all get the supports and resources your child needs to access the general education curriculum like every other student.

6.   Signing the IEP: signing the IEP at the end of the meeting is not necessary at that moment, nor should you be pressured into it. You absolutely may go home, sleep on it, discuss it, and sign the next day, or even days later. You may want to read through it again, notate questions, rewrite goals, etc. **NOTE: not all states require your signature to move forward with implementation of the IEP.** If you have issues or questions, be sure to email within 24–48 hours those questions or concerns or request a second part of the meeting be scheduled.

7.   In the state of Kansas: all IEP meetings are scheduled to be 45 minutes long. This indicates that the team is communicating ahead of time, is working as a team, and is doing a lot of the work in advance. This is a GREAT goal to have! This allows the actual IEP meeting to be short and simple. I suggest this as a part of your team IEP goals. **NOTE: This is in a perfect world. Don't hesitate to have 2–4 meetings to complete the IEP.** Be strong. Be the voice for your child and push for what they need.

8.   Try to be professional: Some parents bring treats and snacks to the meeting; that is up to you. Remember a little honey

goes a long way. Remember that these teachers went into teaching to help children. Underneath the gruff exterior of that teacher, there may be fear and worry about failure! If you can relieve that fear, you can find a way to go forward together! **Best of luck on your next IEP!**

IEP Accommodation List Suggestions

Michelle Tetschner

- Use the word no minimally
- Use PRAISE and excited gestures for success
- Peer Modeling
- Refrain from negative comments
- Reduce visual /auditory distractions
- Simplify fine motor activities
- Provide manipulatives
- Modified writing paper
- Provide opportunities for movement
- Utilize physical modeling when needed
- Provide visual model
- Place marker use for reading assignments
- Provide model / specific examples / demonstrations
- Verbalize information as it is being written on the board
- Emphasize major points/main ideas
- Gain child's attention before speaking
- Use short clear distinctive directions
- Repeat/rephrase/simplify directions/instructions
- Wait 9 seconds before repeating instructions
- Provide opportunities for oral participation

- Scribe writing assignments when appropriate (journal entry, lengthy writing assignments)

- Preferential seating- Especially when copying

- Provide short/immediate breaks

- Reduce assignments, classwork, homework

- A separate location or study carrel

- Read directions, Repeat directions, clarify directions as needed

- More breaks and/or several shorter sessions

- Small group administration or one-on-one testing

- Read aloud the writing prompt, mathematics test items, or science test items

- Write answers directly into test booklet

- Fine-motor/sensory activity prior to writing activities.

- Reduce visual /auditory distractions

- Simplify fine motor activities

- Provide visual model

- Assistance during lunch period (not hovering)

- Provide model / specific examples / demonstrations

- Repeat/rephrase/simplify directions/instructions

- Provide short/immediate feedback

Inclusion Resources

Those who speak on Inclusion:
Julie Causton
Paula Kluth
Torrie Dunlap
Michael Boyle
Cindy May
Richard Villa
Doug Fisher
Dan Habib
Nicole Erdict
Patrick Schwarz

Resources
Special Ed Advocate
Understood.org
Different Roads to Learning
Think Inclusive
TheARC.org
NDSS NDSC IDSC Global DS LuMind
GiGi's Playhouse
Visions and Voices Together FB
Maryland Coalition for Inclusive Ed
TASH
SWIFT Schools
Think College.net
BookShare.com
Austin and Lilly
HSLD.org
Teachers Pay Teachers
PreSchool Prep

IEP Help
   Wrightslaw
   Goal Book

Catholic Resources
   National Catholic Board on Full Inclusion
   FIRE Foundation of Kansas City
   Catholic Coalition for Special Education
   Mustard Seed Conference
   Karen Gaffney-self advocate

Books
   How to teach a child with Down syndrome Math
   How to teach a child with Down syndrome to Read
   Stars (for aides)
   Wrightslaw

Videos To Watch
   Just Like You video
   Frank Stephens video speaking to senate
   Spread the Word to End the Word
   More Alike Than Different
   We All Belong(abicommunity.org)
   Shelly Moore bowling analogy video
   Including Samuel by Dan Habib
   Intelligent Lives by Dan Habib
   Including Isaac/Kala Project

Acknowledgments

There are so many people to say thank you to and the greatest goes to each of the authors that have been willing to share their trials, tribulations and especially their successes in creating inclusive opportunities for themselves and others. We are proud and thankful to each of you for leading the path towards inclusion.

A big thank you to Carrie Clark and NorthStarPaths.com for sharing their visuals to enhance the book as well as our amazing graphic designer Darja Filipovic.

A special thank you to our editor Janet Schaaf who worked diligently to be very gentle with each story, so as to keep the original meaning in each author's own words while creating a book the flows so beautifully. Kudos go to Darcy and especially to Sue Balcer who patiently helped lay out the interior of the book aligning with my vision and dreams. Sue also came to the rescue and helped finish up the cover-she has been a wonder to us!

A special shout out goes to my crew of story reviewers Dianna Haedt, Naomi Haedt, Lisa LaValle, Stephen Tetschner, Jen Tetschner and Jessica Crain. I'm so grateful to each of you!

We are truly grateful for the positive support and encouragement that we received from our friends! We love you all!

And finally-HUGE hugs and love go to Carrie Ro for being the voice of encouragement for Michelle along this journey and being so giving of her valuable time to talk ideas, inspiration and all things inclusion; while always providing endless words of support.

CPSIA information can be obtained
at www.ICGtesting.com
Printed in the USA
LVHW081507281021
701816LV00014B/463